THE CHICAGO CUB *shot for love*

A SHOWGIRL'S CRIME OF PASSION AND THE 1932 WORLD SERIES

JACK BALES

Foreword by Tim Wiles

Published by The History Press
Charleston, SC
www.historypress.com

Front cover, top left: author's collection; *top right*: author's collection; *middle*: author's collection; *bottom*: Associated Press.
Back cover, top: Christina A. Reynen; *bottom*: Wikimedia Commons.

First published 2021

Manufactured in the United States

ISBN 9781467148481

Library of Congress Control Number: 2021934142

Notice: The information in this book is true and complete to the best of our knowledge. It is offered without guarantee on the part of the author or The History Press. The author and The History Press disclaim all liability in connection with the use of this book.

For all my friends at the University of Mary Washington

In a way you might say that young lady triggered all the historic events of the '32 series, including the Babe Ruth called shot.

—*Baseball player Dick Bartell,* Rowdy Richard: A Firsthand Account of the National League Baseball Wars of the 1930s and the Men Who Fought Them *(1987)*

CONTENTS

Foreword, by Tim Wiles 9
Acknowledgements 15
Introduction 19

1. A Jilted Lover Seeks Revenge 23
2. Aftermath of the "Now Famous Hotel Carlos Gunplay" 33
3. "The Girl Who Shot for Love" 45
4. Violet's Troubled Past 55
5. Just "One Thing After Another" for the Cubs 63
6. Playing Hard and Playing to Win 79
7. Last Years 100

Abbreviations 111
Notes 113
Bibliography 135
Index 139
About the Author 143

FOREWORD

Baseball, of course, has the longest and most intriguing history of American team sports. Going hand in hand with that are the game's many cultural touchpoints—its literature, film, connections to American history, culture and politics. Baseball itself is one long story, told in daily chapters ever since the middle of the nineteenth century.

Yesterday, I opened my Yahoo account and clicked on a headline about a former minor-league player, Brandon Martin, convicted of the triple murder of his father, uncle and another man, committed with a baseball bat engraved with his own name. Hmmm. I did not immediately connect that contemporary story with the story told in these pages, but on reflection, they do have several things in common, and some key differences.

Most baseball fans, from the casual to the sophisticated, have probably seen the movie *The Natural*, a cinematographic masterpiece from 1984. Many have also read the 1952 Bernard Malamud novel that inspired the film. Both works have an air of mystery, nostalgia and intrigue, connected to the mysterious shooting of our hero, Roy Hobbs. Some even realize that that shooting, like many details in the book, was probably inspired by real-life events.

Some twenty thousand American males have played in the major leagues, and probably two hundred million have aspired to do so at some point in their lives. As the great book *The Great American Baseball Card Flipping, Trading and Bubble Gum Book* wisely notes, "In 1955, there were 77,263,127 male American human beings. And every one of them in his heart of hearts would have given two arms, a leg and his collection of Davy Crockett iron-ons to be Teddy Ballgame." Ted Williams was a "natural" if ever there was one, albeit one not tinged with a gruesome backstory, unless you count the fact that his severed head now sits in a cryogenic lab in Arizona, in the Splendid Splinter's hope (or perhaps his now deceased, and also frozen, son's) for even more immortality than he has already earned in American culture.

Yet of those twenty thousand men, only two, to my knowledge, have been shot by women scorned. That both shootings happened in Chicago hotel rooms and involved the Cubs is somewhat remarkable. That both shootings happened when the Phillies were in town, even more so. That both men played for the Cubs, and in fact were teammates for two years (though Waitkus had become a Phillie before being shot)—well, just wow.

Some devoted students of the game know that Eddie Waitkus of the Philadelphia Phillies, a former Cub, was shot three years before Malamud's novel was written, in a Chicago hotel room, by a deranged fan named Ruth Ann Steinhagen. Given the timing of the crime and the novel, it is a natural assumption that this inspired Malamud to include such an incident in his novel, and it may well have.

True scholars of the game, and of the Cubs, like retired librarian and author Jack Bales, point out that the Waitkus incident itself may have been inspired by a startlingly similar event a few years prior, in which star Cub shortstop Billy Jurges was shot by a jilted lover, in room 509 of Chicago's Hotel Carlos, just a few blocks north of Wrigley Field.

How bizarre, astonishing and intriguing is it that two Cub players, teammates in 1946–47, were both shot in local hotel rooms by women with a real or imaginary bone to pick? How are these stories not more widely known?

The Jurges shooting in July 1932, as Cubs historian Ed Hartig observes in these pages, "opened the door" for former New York Yankee shortstop Mark Koenig to join the Cubs, inadvertently leading to one of baseball's greatest moments—which may or may not have happened. Koenig joined the Cubs for the pennant race in the wake of Jurges's absence while recovering from the shooting. He contributed mightily to the Cubs' offense over thirty-three games, but when the pennant-winning Cubs met to divvy up the World Series money, they voted him only a half share. Babe Ruth seized on this less than generous decision and rode the Cubs as cheapskates during the series, while they rode him back in other ways. The feud reached its peak in the fifth inning of Game Three at Wrigley Field, when Ruth allegedly "called his shot," predicting a home run off Charlie Root, still the Cubs' winningest pitcher of all time. Entire books have been written on that moment, which happened because Violet Popovich shot Billy Jurges.

One reason the story has remained undertold is that our beloved game has a distressing tendency to tell just about half of its stories, making its male players larger than life and preferring the stories to reside more on the field than off. Yet these players didn't shoot themselves—though sadly, other players have. Both Ruth Ann Steinhagen and Violet Popovich were women, and baseball stories, indeed baseball itself, has a third rail or an invisible wall when it comes to the distaff side. Like the foul line that Dr. Archibald Graham cannot cross in another great baseball book/film, *Shoeless Joe/Field of Dreams*, baseball so often stops short of embracing and revealing its feminine side, the yin to its yang, the other half of the story.

There are as many women in baseball history as there are men. So often we think we know the men who are our baseball heroes, because we know what they did between the foul lines and the basic biographical details of their lives. Yet in many cases, they are shaped and influenced by the women in their lives as much or more than by any other factor. Think of Lou Gehrig's devotion to his mother and later to his wife, Eleanor. We don't often think of those two women when we think of the great Gehrig, yet once you start to study the man, they are giant influences, keys to the puzzle of his quietly intriguing life. What would we still like to know from Marilyn Monroe about Joe DiMaggio? What will Jennifer Lopez tell us in the future about Alex Rodriguez? There's always more to the story on the feminine side.

Over the last generation or two, many more women have begun writing about the game, and many male writers are realizing that there are two sides to every story. There is no denying that an aspiring showgirl, starved for attention and trying to make her way on looks and chutzpah perhaps more than talent, who shoots a star ballplayer in a desperate, film noir–esque bid for not just his attention but also ours, is an intriguing story. But until now, it has been a story not fully told, not fully realized and documented for the ages.

Jack Bales is the writer for the job. A gentleman, a scholar, a librarian, a talented writer, a son of Chicago who has loved the Cubs his whole life, Jack knew a good story when he came upon it. As only a librarian really can, he fully exhausted the print sources on Violet Popovich and Billy Jurges and took from them a narrative that he then fleshed out with photographs, archival records, genealogical resources and interviews with family members

Chicago Cubs corporate secretary Margaret Donahue, the first woman to rise to an executive position in Major League Baseball, and club president William Veeck pore over ticket requests for the 1929 World Series at Wrigley Field. *Margaret Donahue family*.

of the tale's two principal players. There is, of course, even more to the story than even Bales has managed to dig up, but any remaining aspects of the tale are not in this book, because they no longer exist. Perhaps out of midcentury propriety, or semi-lurid shame, or because journalists at the time told the story mostly from a baseball point of view, there is much we will never know hinted at in these pages.

But what is written here is fascinating, detailed, entertainingly told and well worth your time. Fifty photographs supplement the text and add to the intrigue. I'd love to be a fly on the wall in a hotel bar sometime in 1946–47, when perhaps Jurges told Waitkus about the shooting, the latter innocent yet of his own 1949 shooting. But if such a conversation ever happened, it has not been recorded. This book is the next best thing.

Tim Wiles is the director of the Guilderland Public Library near Albany, New York, where he lives with his family. From 1995 to 2014, he was the research director of the National Baseball Hall of Fame Library in Cooperstown. He co-edited *Line Drives: 100 Contemporary Baseball Poems* and co-authored *Baseball's Greatest Hit: The Story of "Take Me Out to the Ball Game."* In his work at the Hall of Fame, he always tried to bring women's perspectives into contemporary research on baseball history.

ACKNOWLEDGEMENTS

Numerous persons have enabled me to complete this book. Tim Wiles is the former research director at the National Baseball Hall of Fame Library and an authority on women in baseball. He read a draft of my work, made suggestions and set the perfect tone with his excellent, thought-provoking foreword. Cubs expert and longtime season ticket holder Raymond D. Kush carefully pored over my manuscript and made numerous comments and corrections that greatly improved the finished product. I am grateful to both of them for their critical eyes and firm hands. The Chicago Cubs' official historian, Ed Hartig, shared with me—as he has for years—his vast knowledge of the team's history.

Mark Prescott, the son of Violet Popovich's brother Mark, provided many of the photographs in this book. Both he and his cousin Michael Prescott recounted stories about their aunt in phone calls, emails and letters. I was pleased to be able to interview Billy Jurges's daughter, Suzanne Price, and her son, Bill Price, and I thank them both for readily answering my questions.

Professional researcher and genealogist Christina A. Reynen tracked down much about Violet Popovich and her family in libraries, archives, court files and databases. Ellen Keith and Lesley Martin of the Chicago History Museum showed me the records of the Uhlich Children's Home, where Violet and her brothers lived for years.

Marshall Philyaw provided a fine, detailed drawing of how the shooting in the Hotel Carlos might have appeared to an onlooker. I am indebted to Art Ahrens, Steve Albertson, Jim Davis, Donald R. Eldred, Bill Gowen,

Bill Hageman, Jim Hall, Mike Hill, Rob Kasper and Tom Wolf for their longtime interest in my research and writing. I also owe a great deal to the fine editorial and production professionals of The History Press.

In the summer of 2020, I retired after more than four decades as the Reference and Humanities Librarian at the University of Mary Washington in Fredericksburg, Virginia. Throughout the years, I have enjoyed the assistance and support of many library and university colleagues. I was able to read various historic newspapers only because Carla Bailey borrowed the microfilm—as well as dozens of other invaluable works—through interlibrary loan. University Librarian Rosemary Arneson made numerous resources available and enabled me to discuss my research at baseball meetings and conferences. Brianne Dort, Andrea Meckley and James Pape helped keep a special microfilm reader-printer running smoothly (and Andrea did the same for my personal computer). Carolyn Parsons and Marianne Brokaw expertly scanned photographs and documents, and Angie White meticulously scanned and enhanced the quality of many of my images. Skilled (and dogged!) genealogist Renee Davis tracked down obscure facts and articles and placed her digital expertise with photographs at my disposal. I have discussed writing projects with Beth Perkins for more than thirty-five years, and I wish her good things, only good things during her retirement years in her home state of Mississippi.

I have always been able to count on my colleagues in the reference department. They helped make my work environment positive, productive and extremely enjoyable. They include Paul Boger, Peter Catlin, Elizabeth Heitsch and Erin Wysong. Other library staff members, both past and present, who have furnished much encouragement and assistance with this book and/or assorted other writing projects include Sarah Appleby, Linda Carver, Suzanne Chase, Ron Comer, Suzanne Crosnicker, Caitlin DeMarco, Karen Duffy, Summer Durrant, Tina Faulconer, Christie Glancy, Bob Grattan, Becky Harris, Shannon Hauser, Tammy Hefner, Donna Hudgins, Pauline Jenkins, Phyllis Johnson, Tim Newman, Sara Parker-Gray, Katherine Perdue, Wanda Pittman, Nicole St. John, Roy Strohl and Olivia Vander Bleek.

Other Mary Washington colleagues and friends who have been particularly helpful and encouraging over the years include Bill Anderson, Rosemary Barra, Anna Billingsley, Porter Blakemore, Joanna Catron, Claudine Ferrell, Steve Gallik, Doug Gately, Edward Gray, Jim Groom, Scott Harris, David and Jean Hunt, Rick Hurley, Milton Kline, Bob MacDonald, Ken Machande, Lisa Marvashti, Jeff McClurken, Nina

Mikhalevsky, Margaret Mock, John Morello, Laura Moyer, Joe Nicholas, Tommy Pack, Troy and Kelly Paino, Tom Riley, Beverley Shelesky, Tom Sheridan, Jerry Slezak, Neva Trenis, Paulette Watson, Marty and Vicky Wilder, Grace Winfield and Grant Woodwell. Bill and Terrie Crawley have for decades assisted me in my professional and personal endeavors, and I am grateful for both their friendship and their fellowship.

My family members have heard stories of my research ever since I first became interested in the captivating chronicle of Billy and Violet. The visual appeal of this book was vastly improved by Kate Bales's expertise with photographs and her care and attention to the slightest detail. Dick Bales was always available to find articles in Chicago libraries and to discuss research and writing questions. Thanks, too, go to Robert, David, Jane, Peggy, Beth, R.J. and Phyllis, as well as to Apiluk, Joanne, Jon and Steve.

And, of course, I gratefully thank Laura and Patrick, who have always been my staunch friends and companions as well as my children.

INTRODUCTION

The day after the Chicago Cubs won the National League pennant, the headline in the sports pages of the September 21, 1932 *Chicago Daily Tribune* summed up the entire season: "Cubs Defy Experts and Hard Luck to Win." The reporter pointed out that in March of that year, only three out of fifty-seven baseball authorities had predicted the Cubs would secure the pennant. "The triumph of the Chicagoans is made all the more surprising," the sportswriter went on, "by the fact that they won despite distractions that not even the sourest prophet had considered in the preparation of their appraisals."

The disruptions were indeed serious ones and included the obvious bad blood between Cubs' president William Veeck and the team's talented but taciturn manager, Rogers Hornsby. Hornsby's troubles—and the corresponding newspaper coverage—only escalated after he found himself embroiled in a front-page gambling scandal that allegedly involved several well-known Cub players. Newspapers and magazines kept baseball fans informed as to what was going on, and in its August 18 issue, *The Sporting News* even provided a timeline and elaborate listing of events in a lengthy article aptly titled "Five Wild Weeks Give the Cubs a Succession of Varied Thrills."

The wildest "thrill"—and the first one on *The Sporting News*'s list—was the July 6 shooting of shortstop Billy Jurges by his jilted lover, former showgirl Violet Popovich. I read about the incident about a decade ago in a few Cub histories, but the authors limited their coverage to just cursory comments.

Since I felt that the strange saga of the showgirl and the shortstop made the Cubs' tumultuous season particularly intriguing, I set out to find additional details about the dramatic confrontation in Jurges's Chicago hotel room—and also about the two persons involved. Information about Billy's life seemed readily available, but what about Violet's background, childhood and family? How did the shooting affect the rest of the Cubs' 1932 season, especially during the pennant race? Could the incident have played a role in the events leading up to the World Series and Babe Ruth's "Called Shot"? I was curious, too, about what happened to Violet after the excitement died down and newspapers turned to other stories. I also wanted to learn more about Jurges's extensive baseball career, particularly after he left the Cubs in 1938.

I managed to find answers to all of my questions. The first chapter of this book describes how the Chicago Cubs were in the middle of a tight pennant race when Violet Popovich (described by one newspaper as a "21-year-old comely brunette") made headlines after she quietly withdrew a revolver from her purse and shot Billy Jurges in room 509 of the Hotel Carlos. As related in chapters 2 and 3, the well-known ballplayer refused to press charges, and Violet quickly saw an opportunity to bill herself as "The Girl Who Shot for Love" and sing in a city burlesque theater. (Management did its part to attract an audience by booking some "Bare Cub Girls" as her opening act.) Violet's childhood years were not particularly happy and carefree ones, as recounted in chapter 4. The fifth chapter is devoted to the Cubs' 1932 season, complete with the "distractions" the *Tribune* brought up. The season ended with the Chicago Cubs–New York Yankees World Series and one of the most famous home runs in baseball history, Babe Ruth's arguable "Called Shot." Chapter 6 focuses on Jurges's career after the 1932 season, while the last chapter chronicles the final years of both him and Popovich.

My research sources include newspapers, magazines, memoirs of players, archival and court records, biographies, baseball histories and specialized online works. I found contemporary newspaper articles to be especially valuable, as they provided interviews not only with Billy Jurges and Violet Popovich but also with other persons significant to the entire narrative. In addition, conversations and correspondence with Jurges and Popovich family members filled in numerous blanks in my research. Dozens of photographs, many of them never before published, complement the text.

Notes at the end of the book, keyed to each chapter, document the works I used in my text and furnish resources for persons desiring additional information. I abbreviate a few often-cited publications, and with the endnotes I include a list of these titles and their abbreviations. Citations to book titles are abbreviated in the endnotes, and full publication information is provided in the bibliography.

—Jack Bales
Fredericksburg, Virginia

I

A JILTED LOVER SEEKS REVENGE

I've been shot. Get a doctor. Get the gun in the other room there. Don't let her get it.
—*Billy Jurges,* Chicago Daily News, *July 6, 1932*

Violet Popovich seldom lacked for male companionship. After all, she was dark-haired, attractive, outgoing and rather statuesque at about five feet, nine inches. She was a "stunning beauty," according to a family member. With her olive complexion, lively gray eyes and confident sense of style, the native Chicagoan enjoyed an active social life with men who were more than happy to escort her to parties and clubs around town. High on her list of eligible bachelors were sports figures. She liked baseball—particularly baseball players—and she fell for handsome Chicago Cubs shortstop Billy Jurges soon after they were introduced. "Bill is the boy in 100,000 for me," twenty-one-year-old Violet exclaimed in the summer of 1932. "I met him at a party a year ago, and if it wasn't love at first sight, it was just about second."

But contrary to Popovich's declaration of devotion, Jurges, age twenty-four, did not view their relationship as "love at first sight"—or second or even third. He certainly appreciated the company of the vivacious young woman with the radiant smile, but he also, as he readily acknowledged, liked being "single, running around and having a lot of fun." Much of that fun in mid-1932 centered on the baseball field. It was his second season with the Chicago Cubs, and Jurges intended to be in the thick of the excitement as the team made a run for the National League pennant.[1]

All appears right in the world of teenager Violet Popovich as she sits in the doorway of a Chicago house. *MA&LJ Prescott Joint Trust.*

The brown-haired young man with brown eyes and a ruddy complexion could barely remember when his life did not revolve around baseball. William Frederick "Billy" Jurges was born on May 9, 1908, in the Bronx in New York, the third child of Frederick H. Jurges, a shipping clerk, and Anna M. Horstmann Jurges. When Billy was two, the family—which eventually included four boys and a girl—moved to the Highland Park area of Brooklyn. Billy played sandlot baseball while growing up, but with a part-time job in high school delivering groceries with a horse and cart, there was little opportunity for him to join the school team. He got his chance to play baseball later on, though, when, after two years of high school, he took a job as a bank messenger. "Maybe it was because I told them I was a ball player," he recalled years later. "The bank had a team and I became a member."

At age seventeen, Jurges played for the semipro Hawtree Indians in South Ozone Park, a neighborhood in the New York City borough of Queens.

As luck would have it, umpire Dick Meehan knew former New York Giant second baseman Billy Gilbert, who was a scout for the Newark (New Jersey) Bears of the International League. Gilbert quickly noticed Jurges's exceptional skills as a baseball player, and he told the young man he would do all he could to help further his career.

Jurges signed a contract with the Bears, and on Gilbert's recommendation, they assigned him to play for the New England League's Manchester (New Hampshire) Blue Sox to gain experience. As Jurges recollected, he first signed as an outfielder for $250 a month. "In 1927, I went to spring training in Manchester….They had three regular outfielders. I could see I wasn't going to play, so I started fooling around shortstop. The manager asked me if I could play there, and I said, 'Sure.' So that's how I became a shortstop in professional ball."[2]

Billy batted .255 for the Blue Sox in 1927 and .332 in 1928. At 175 pounds and five feet, eleven and a half inches tall, Jurges was among the league's best hitters, and in 1928, he was chosen Most Valuable Player. A baseball scout had seen Billy play and recommended him to the Chicago Cubs, who bought the right-handed shortstop for $5,000. "He is fast and covers acres of ground to either side of him," a sportswriter observed shortly before Jurges reported to the Cubs in the summer of 1928. "He

1927
PLAYER
Jurges, W. F.
INFORMATION CARD 1930
HEILBRONER BASEBALL BUREAU FORT WAYNE, IND.
25 26-27-28-29
CLUB Manchester
POSITION Short Stop
BATS RH OR LH Right Handed
THROWS RH OR LH Do
AGE 19 MONTH 5 DAY 9 YEAR 1908
HEIGHT 5' 11
WEIGHT 168
CLUB WITH 1926 —
WRITE YOUR FULL NAME AND PERMANENT OR WINTER ADDRESS
NAME Wm. F. Jurges
STREET 296 Arlington Ave.
CITY N.Y.
STATE N.Y.
1928 275 Arlington Ave Brooklyn N.Y.

The Heilbroner Baseball Bureau collected data by sending each ballplayer an informational card, which he would fill out and return. The bureau regularly updated the cards. *Author's collection.*

fields the ball smoothly, knows how to get in front of hard shots and gets his throws away fast with his powerful arm."

Chicago sent Billy to play for the Reading (Pennsylvania) Keystones, the Cubs' Double-A team in the International League, where he hit .256 in 1929 and .288 in 1930. "Two years elapsed before they remembered I was there," Jurges recalled, but he soon got his chance to play major-league baseball. In 1931, he worked out with the Cubs during spring training on Santa Catalina Island, a resort area in the Pacific just off the coast of southern California.

The Chicago Cubs' manager, Rogers Hornsby, liked what he saw as he scrutinized the young player during pre-season exhibition games. "I consider Jurges one of the finest prospects in recent years," he told a sportswriter, and the manager let Jurges take the field during a May 4, 1931 game against the Cincinnati Reds. The *Chicago Daily Tribune* wrote in its game-day coverage that "the fact that the Cubs were leading 13 to 0 at the end of the seventh [inning] caused Manager Hornsby to…give the fans their first look at Bill Jurges, the sensational but heretofore idle young infielder who performed so brilliantly in spring training.…The first play after Bill got in the game was a grounder which gave the youthful star a chance to display his rifle arm."[3]

Jurges played in eighty-eight games that season and finished his rookie year with a .201 batting average. After Cub shortstop Woody English fractured his right index finger in late March 1932, Billy took over his duties; English moved over to third base. After a solid start in his second season in the majors, Jurges was "playing brilliantly," as reported in the *New York Times*. *The Sporting News* considered his fielding "a defensive masterpiece," adding that Jurges's expertise impelled "no less an authority on infielding than his manager, Hornsby, to declare that Bill is the best shortstop in the game."[4]

Starry-eyed Violet Popovich undoubtedly thought so, too, but the baseball-obsessed Jurges was likely more interested in his batting average and keeping his place on the team than in the smitten young woman. Undaunted, the former stage actress saw her chance to continue the relationship when she went to New York in May to pursue her acting career. Although she found work only as a model for "confession" magazines, she was able to cheer Billy from the stands at Ebbets Field when the Cubs traveled east on a road trip and took on the Brooklyn Dodgers.

Violet even got to see firsthand Billy's competitive nature and fiery spirit. Tempers were high on June 9 after a Dodger player sliding into

Shortstop Billy Jurges played for the Chicago Cubs from 1931 to 1938 and from 1946 to 1947. This photograph was taken in 1934. *Author's collection.*

second base tried to drive his spiked shoe into Jurges's left leg. Billy deftly sidestepped to avoid getting injured, but Dodger infielder Neal Finn was not so lucky a few innings later, when Cub hurler Jakie May—in apparent payback—hit him squarely on the arm with a pitched ball.

The animosity between the teams was carried over into the game the next day. "Baseball was merely incidental," observed the *Chicago Daily*

Tribune, as the angry ballplayers "went in for a bigger and better show." The game was barely underway when Finn, scurrying for second base, tried to run into Jurges. Billy easily eluded him and retaliated with a few derisive comments. Finn "leaped for the Cub youngster and delivered a right and left in the direction of the chin. Where the blows actually landed was a question, but impartial critics insisted they landed harmlessly on Jurges' shoulder." The benches emptied and punches flew, though Jurges ended up with only a small scratch on the side of his face. He and Finn were each fined $100 for their part in the "battle royal between the two clubs," as one sportswriter phrased it.

This was not Billy's first baseball brawl, nor would it be the last. "His belligerent eagerness to win has drawn him into more than one fist fight on the field," a sportswriter remarked a few years later. "Bill passes over his battles lightly and holds no grudges. He says, 'They just come up in the heat of the game when everyone is on edge, and I forget about them as soon as they are over.'"

Perhaps Jurges did not brush aside this particular fight so quickly. Violet, fascinated, had watched the fisticuffs from the stands and proudly wrote to her brother Mike that she had played a small part in it all by helping to calm Billy down after the game. She may have exaggerated her role, however. It was well known around the Chicago ballpark that Violet often waited for Billy after games, and as he left the clubhouse, she would grasp his arm and try to engage him in conversation.

If Jurges did indeed appreciate her concern, he apparently hid it well. She telephoned him several times at his Brooklyn home, but his parents sensed little romantic interest on his part. "Bill talked to her but didn't seem at all anxious about her," his father said. "He never was a so-called ladies' man. Since he was a little boy his only love has been baseball."[5]

Billy and Violet quarreled and broke up while they were in New York, and she remained in the city while the Cubs continued their road trip. The team came home following a 4–1 loss to the St. Louis Cardinals on June 27. Popovich returned to Chicago on July 3 and took a room at the Hotel Carlos, where she often resided while in the city. Since the small residential hotel at 3834 Sheffield Avenue (now North Sheffield) was just a couple blocks north of Wrigley Field, the Cubs' ballpark, Jurges and some of his teammates, including outfielders Marv Gudat, Vince Barton and Kiki Cuyler, also stayed there during the summer months.

The ballplayers were at the hotel on Wednesday morning, July 6, as the Cubs were set to open a three-game series that afternoon against

A postcard of the Hotel Carlos from the early 1930s. Billy Jurges's corner room fronted the street on the right side of the top floor. *Author's collection.*

the Philadelphia Phillies. It was bright and sunny out—a good day for a baseball game. Popovich was staying in room 111, and after calling Jurges at 9:45 to say she wanted to see him, she went upstairs about a half hour later and knocked on room 509. With a casual, almost indifferent, air, Billy opened the door, and she walked in. They had not talked in days, and before long the two began arguing again. Although she wanted to get back together with him, he made it clear that baseball took precedence over his social life—and her. "I'm not going to go out on any more dates," he said emphatically. "We've got a chance to win the pennant. I've got to get my rest."

Jurges's words only fueled her smoldering anger, and as they continued to fight, she asked for a glass of water. While he went to get it, she opened her purse and drew out a small revolver. He came back with the glass, saw the gun and quickly tried to grab it. As the two struggled for the weapon, three shots were fired. One bullet entered Jurges's right side, deflected off a rib and came out his right shoulder. A second struck his left hand. After a third bullet hit Popovich's left hand, went up about six inches and lodged in her arm, Jurges managed to wrench the gun from her and toss it aside as he awkwardly stumbled into a nearby chair.[6]

Billy's teammates were preparing to leave for the ballpark when they heard the gunshots. Gudat was the first one to reach the scene.

"I found Bill sprawled across a chair in his room, holding his side," Gudat said. "The girl was standing nearby."

"I've been shot," Jurges said. "Get a doctor."

The young woman dashed over and threw herself on Jurges, but he pushed her away. Barton entered the room, and Gudat left him to look after Jurges while he ran to the lobby for help.

Jurges told Barton, "Get the gun in the other room there. Don't let her get it." Barton ran to pick up the revolver where Jurges had thrown it after wrestling it from Popovich.

The Cubs' team physician, Dr. John C. Davis, happened to be at the Hotel Carlos that morning, and he treated both Billy and Violet. Billy later remembered he had been "bleeding like a pig," but his injuries were not as bad as they looked. His rib had prevented a bullet from passing through his abdomen, which probably saved his life, and Davis said that he would be able to get back on the baseball field in two or three weeks. Jurges and Popovich were both taken to the Illinois Masonic Hospital on Wellington Avenue, less than two miles from the hotel.

An artist imagines the scene in the Hotel Carlos when an angry Violet Popovich pulls a gun from her purse and confronts a startled Billy Jurges. *Marshall Philyaw.*

At the hospital, Popovich told police that "I wanted to marry him. I went to his room to commit suicide."

Lieutenant William J. O'Brien interrogated her. "What were you doing in Jurges' room?"

"I went there to kill myself," she repeated.

"Why didn't you do the job in your own room?" O'Brien demanded.

"I won't say," she replied.

"What's your reason for suicide?"

"Private reasons," she snapped back.

Violet Popovich, her left arm bandaged, is escorted from a police patrol wagon to the hospital unit of Chicago's Bridewell Prison. *Author's collection.*

Popovich's wound was superficial, and the next day, she was moved to the hospital at Chicago's Bridewell Prison, located on Twenty-Sixth Street and California Avenue. Although Violet had told the police she had only wanted to shoot herself, they obviously did not believe her. And as it turned out, she had more problems than just a minor injury to her arm. Instead of being bandaged up, released and allowed to go home, she found herself in custody—booked on a charge of assault with intent to kill.[7]

2

AFTERMATH OF THE "NOW FAMOUS HOTEL CARLOS GUNPLAY"

I didn't intend to kill Bill. That was farthest from my mind.
—Violet Popovich, (Chicago) Daily Illustrated Times, *July 7, 1932*

The sensational shooting of a popular baseball player by his former lover immediately captured the public's attention. Newspaper readers clamored to find out exactly what happened in room 509 of Chicago's Hotel Carlos, and editors "stopped the presses," as the expression goes, to quickly provide page-one details. Just a few hours after reporters first heard the news, Chicago's *Daily Illustrated Times* was on the newsstands with a banner headline: "Bill Jurges Shot by Spurned Cabaret Girl." The *Chicago Daily News* also hit the streets that afternoon, its front page lit up with "Jurges, Star Cub, Is Shot," followed by "Girl Wounded in Hotel Mystery; Both Will Live." The Associated Press carried the news across the country, reporting that "a woman scorned almost took the life of Bill Jurges, star shortstop of the Chicago National Baseball Club."

When police questioned that scorned woman, she admitted that the gun was hers and that the shots were fired "in a scuffle." She told officers her name was Violet Valli, but it did not take them long to figure out that that was a stage name. In a search of her hotel room they found on her luggage the name Violet Popovich of 743 Belden Avenue, the Chicago home address of her mother, Margaret Heindl. Violet was reportedly divorced from one Tony Stenella, whom she claimed deserted her on May 3, 1929. She said she was employed as a cashier in a cigar store on the city's North Side.[8]

This photograph of Violet Popovich was found in her Chicago hotel room after she shot baseball player Billy Jurges. *Author's collection.*

Besides luggage, officers found several empty liquor bottles in Violet's hotel room, as well as a few photographs of her. One photo was a studio portrait, her short dark hair framing her smiling face. There was also a farewell letter addressed to one of her brothers, who worked at a local YMCA on Division Street. The letter revealed that there was more to the lovers' breakup than Billy simply wanting to get more rest.

> *Dear Mike:*
> *I have just a few more minutes of waiting before I see Billy, so I'll write and try to explain everything. I know you'll understand.*
> *To me life without Billy isn't worth living, but why should I leave this earth alone? I'm going to take Billy with me. We are getting along famously, just as everything should go, but a few people like Ki-Ki* [sic] *Cuyler and Lew Steadman forgot that there might be anything fine and beautiful in our love for each other and dragged it in the mud. I know what I'm doing is best for me and I hate to do it—but????*
> *My last wish is that mother, you and the boys go to California and enjoy life to the greatest extent, and remember your father once in a while. I can't write any more. I'm so nervous. I love all of you.*
> *Violet*[9]

Popovich claimed after her arrest that the threatening letter was simply the result of "too much gin." She said of Jurges that "I loved him and I thought he loved me" and insisted she really had intended just to shoot herself "to make Bill sorry" for breaking up with her:

> *I'm lucky—and how!—that the shots were not serious. I was just out of my mind—that's all—mostly due to drinking…I didn't intend to kill Bill. That was farthest from my mind. That goes for the rest of the note too—about Cuyler and all that. I don't see how they can charge me with anything. I didn't mean to hurt anybody else and it's my business if I wanted to kill myself, isn't it? Bill was just trying to keep me from shooting myself.*[10]

Violet wrote a letter to Jurges, which her brother Mike delivered to him. Addressed to "Billy Darling," she pleaded with him to "please think kindly of me. Don't hate me too much, Billy. If I hadn't cared so much things would never have happened like they did. Forgive me." She was pleased that he wrote back to say he would do anything he could to help her.

And Billy did help. He told reporters from his hospital bed that he thought a great deal of Violet and would not press charges against her or sign a complaint. That was a huge relief to her, though she still faced arraignment in felony court on July 8. One of her attorneys, Herbert G. Immenhausen, explained to Judge John A. Sbarbaro that Popovich was under police guard in her hospital room and could not appear in court. Judge Sbarbaro responded that bond would be fixed at $7,500 and he would schedule the case for July 15. He added: "I understand that Bill Jurges has declined to prosecute the defendant. I want it understood that if he retains this attitude I shall issue a subpoena for his appearance as a witness."

Jurges had even refused to talk to his parents about Violet, and he shook his head when he heard what Sbarbaro had decided. "Gee, I don't see why the judge wants to be that way," he said. "I certainly don't want to prosecute Violet. I have no doubt that she shot me accidentally, she only wanted to kill herself and I tried to stop her. If I'm made to appear in court, that's all I can say about the affair."

Newspaper reporters, however, had plenty to say about what one of them called the "now famous Hotel Carlos gunplay." As photographers barged into Popovich's hospital room to take pictures of her lying in bed, she covered her face with her uninjured right arm while flashbulbs popped before her. "Violet dislikes cameras," a reporter wrote as a caption, adding

John A. Sbarbaro, the judge in the Billy Jurges–Violet Popovich case, presents a copy of his book, *Marriage Is on Trial*, to a young woman. *Author's collection.*

that she "went into a one-woman huddle" when the cameraman walked in on her. She was referred to in stories as a "dark-haired former show girl," "21-year-old comely brunette," "pretty gun-toter," "spurned sweetheart" and "chestnut haired divorcée."[11]

Violet Popovich was married at age eighteen, at about the time this photograph was taken of her and her mother, Margaret. *MA&LJ Prescott Joint Trust.*

A *Chicago American* journalist described how "the raven-tressed beauty tossed in her bed as she tore the curtain of secrecy from her troubled romance with Bill Jurges." She talked about her personal life, as well, revealing that she had married at age eighteen after "one of those puppy love affairs with a schoolboy." The marriage was doomed right from the beginning, she said. "I never lived with him and we were divorced six months later." In late 1929, she had taken dance lessons at the Ned Wayburn studio in Chicago, which led her to the chorus of *Earl Carroll Vanities*. This series of stage musicals, directed by theatrical producer Earl Carroll between 1923 and 1940, featured dance revues, burlesque performances, comedy routines and risqué sketches.

Violet had left Carroll's employment by the time she met Cub outfielder Hazen Shirley "Kiki" Cuyler in early 1931. During interviews, she said he had been "very attentive," but when she found out he was married, "I had nothing more to do with him." Later that year, Billy Jurges entered her life. He represented stability, something certainly lacking in her home life, and she felt that at long last she had found the person and the affectionate, caring relationship she had always wanted. "Such a personality!" she exclaimed. "Such a man!...I love Bill Jurges for himself—and not for his place in the public eye or his popularity."

She related that at first the two of them got along very well and spent quite a bit of time together. That changed, though, when his friends began to tell him—falsely, she said—that she was seeing other men and he should break up with her. "Gossips began to cast aspersions on my character," Violet hotly declared, and "I could see that Bill's ardor was waning." Her mood and spirits, though, soon lifted. She and a young woman named Betty went to New York in May to find work on the stage, and when the Cubs were in town during their road trip, "Bill called me up. I was enthralled." They went out several times in New York, but "in Chicago those terrible stories again crept up to destroy our love affair. I was frantic."

Violet knew that Billy was beginning to believe all the rumors, so she made plans to see him after both she and the Cubs were back in Chicago:

> *I called him on the telephone—we both live in the same hotel—and went up to see him. I sent Bill for a glass of water and when he went out of the room I pulled out my revolver, intending to kill myself. Bill saw me and grabbed the gun.*
>
> *We fought for it. We really fought for it. The gun kept exploding. I didn't want to hurt him.*[12]

Violet maintained she had wanted to shoot herself—not Jurges—to prove to her boyfriend that she loved him and had been "a good girl." It was all the fault of Jurges's friend Lew Steadman and other malicious talebearers, she emphasized, particularly Kiki Cuyler. Reporters asked Cuyler to comment on Violet's allegations, and he denied that he had ever dated her nor that he had interfered with her romance with Jurges. "Miss Valli's charge that I had any influence over Jurges is absurd," he said. "I haven't seen her but once or twice in three years, and that was to autograph scorecards. The only thing I ever told Jurges was to attend to business and he'd be a star."

Cuyler's denial notwithstanding, Jurges admitted that his married teammate was a "big ladies' man" and that Popovich had indeed gone out with Cuyler, as well as with other ballplayers. One of them was Leo Durocher, then a shortstop with the Cincinnati Reds. Durocher was well known as something of a ladies' man himself, and he frequently "angered husbands, fathers, and boyfriends," according to a biographer. Another man she saw was Al Lopez, a catcher with the Brooklyn Dodgers, who told Jurges that Popovich had a "bad reputation."[13]

But it was Cuyler's disparaging remarks about her that particularly gnawed at Violet on the morning of July 6, 1932. More than fifty years later, Jurges remembered that "I took the rap for it, but she had gone to Cuyler's room first....She had the key to his room but he wasn't there. She wrote a note and put it on the mirror: 'I'M GOING TO KILL YOU!'"

Jurges's story of Popovich leaving a note on Cuyler's mirror does not appear in any of the newspaper accounts of the shooting. Her fury, though, had definitely been noticed by residents of the Hotel Carlos, who heard her exclaim on July 5 that she would "get Jurges" and also shoot Cuyler because "he was always interfering." She even let it be known among Cub players that she was a spurned woman and intended to do something about it. Jurges in fact had been warned of her threats and advised to leave the hotel, but he had shrugged off the possibility that Violet might actually harm him. What had angered her even more was the anonymous telegram she received that intimated Jurges had been out with other women. A resident of the hotel had overheard Violet blurt out to a friend, "If he denies this I'll forgive him. Otherwise I'll give him the works." Another hotel guest reported that on the evening of July 5, Violet and her friend had gone out target shooting in the alley behind the hotel.[14]

While police looked for the unknown young woman, Popovich continued to rest and recover in the hospital. She was strong enough on July 9 to be transferred from Bridewell's hospital unit to the jail. Later that day, her church minister, Jacob Pister of St. Paul's Evangelical and Reformed Church, arranged for a parishioner to post her $7,500 bond. Pister also saw to it that she could recuperate in a small private hospital affiliated with the church. For her part, Violet successfully pleaded with him to be allowed to return to the church choir, where as a young girl she had spent numerous hours singing hymns during Sunday services.

With her medical, legal and even spiritual needs presumably in order, Violet's thoughts turned to trying to see Billy. She first called his mother in Brooklyn. "From her voice," Violet told reporters, "Mrs. Jurges must be an awfully sweet woman. I'd surely like to meet her. And Bill—well, he's a pretty square fellow for not wanting to prosecute me." She wanted to talk with him, but his physician and friends ruled otherwise and refused to give their permission. Jurges continued to convalesce at the Illinois Masonic Hospital, where his own thoughts focused not on her, but on the Cubs. Although he wished Violet well, he had no desire to speak with the woman who had both threatened and shot him. He instead chatted amiably with reporters, remarking that he wished he could play baseball but was glad that at least he could listen to the games on the radio in his hospital room.

Cubs president William Veeck and team manager Rogers Hornsby also looked forward to having their star infielder out of the hospital and back on the field. "Jurges unquestionably is one of the finest shortstops in the majors today," Hornsby said, "and his loss at this time, when we are in the heat of the pennant fight comes as a great blow." Happily, on July 10, Dr. Davis allowed Billy to go to the ballpark, where he watched the Cubs defeat the Boston Braves, 4–0.[15]

Jurges left the hospital three days later and worked out a bit with his teammates. "Hope to get back in the game in a day or two at the latest," he told reporters. "Feeling fine and am crazy to play ball again." While sitting in the Cubs' dugout that day, he was served a subpoena, and although he agreed to appear in court, he declared once again that he would not testify against his former girlfriend. He had not talked to her since the shooting, but the next day, he very well may have seen her. At the same time that he was in the Cubs' dugout watching his teammates play the Brooklyn Dodgers, Violet was in the stands watching him. "She sat near the Brooklyn dugout," wrote a sportswriter, "but had a view of the open side of the Cub dugout in which sat her favorite target, Bill Jurges."

The ballplayer was anxious to put his messy, public love life behind him. As it turned out, Judge Sbarbaro was the ideal person to make the entire matter quietly disappear, as he was not only a Cub fan but also the consummate political "fixer." Incredibly, at the same time that he served the public as a judge and attorney, he ran a mortuary favored by Chicago's mobsters, who used its garage as a drop-off spot for bootleg liquor. He was "on the take," as one Chicago historian bluntly affirmed, and "when he wasn't putting gangsters in jail, he was putting them in coffins." After his funeral home at 708 North Wells Street was bombed in 1928, more than a few reporters had raised their eyebrows in disbelief when he lamely explained that he had recently given "heavy punishment to gamblers brought before me....Perhaps they did it."[16]

Jurges was present in Judge Sbarbaro's courtroom on July 15, tastefully attired in a gray suit and a colorful "tapestry-effect tie." Violet's mother and the young woman's showgirl friends sat anxiously in the packed courtroom. Also present were "baseball fans, girl romanticists and mere thrill-seekers," as well as cameramen, from whom Jurges covered his face with a handkerchief. When Violet entered the courtroom shortly after 9:00 a.m. with her two

Violet Popovich, with bandaged arm, in court on July 15, 1932, alongside attorneys Herbert G. Immenhausen (*left*) and James M. Burke. *Bill Hageman.*

attorneys, former judge Herbert G. Immenhausen and James M. Burke, "The crowd gasped at her radiant beauty."

Part of their astonishment may have been due to her fashionable outfit. Violet wore a white felt hat with a white patent-leather strap. She was a "symphony in red and white," noted one observer, "with her red earrings, red shoes, and red striped trimmings on her white crepe sports dress exactly matching her shade of lipstick." Her red belt was "worn rather high."

When the case was called, Violet Popovich, her two attorneys, Billy Jurges, policeman Michael Fay and Assistant State's Attorney Russell Root stepped before Judge John A. Sbarbaro's bench. A completely composed Violet stood smiling in front of the judge, her left arm bandaged from wrist to elbow. Jurges, his left hand wrapped up, "twisted about nervously, as he stood a[bo]ut two feet from his old sweetheart before the bench."

Officer Fay testified that he had gone to the Hotel Carlos on July 6 in response to a police call and found Violet Popovich lying across the bed in room 509, Jurges's room. She told him that she had called Billy from the hotel at 9:45 a.m. and went to his room. "She said she had words with him and then [the] shooting happened," Fay testified.

"Did she tell you there was a struggle for the gun and shots were fired?" asked Root.

"Yes," said Fay.

Then Judge Sbarbaro called Jurges to give his testimony.

"Your honor," he said, "I have no desire to testify against this woman."

"You don't want to prosecute?" asked the judge.

"No," said Jurges.

"But you've been subpoenaed," said Root. Jurges remained silent.

"You've no reason to expect any more trouble from this woman?" asked the judge.

"No," replied Jurges.

"Let it be recorded," said the judge, "that this case is dismissed for want of prosecution." He paused for a moment and then continued. "Let's hope no more ball players are shot."

Jurges had privately told Sbarbaro beforehand that he wanted to forget the whole matter, and as the judge's final words rang out, Jurges smiled and walked out of the courtroom. During the half-hour hearing, neither he nor Popovich appeared to even notice each other. Violet, accompanied by her two attorneys, stepped into the press room, where she told newspaper reporters that her romance with Jurges was over and she had no intention of contacting him. "I owe it to my self-respect to consider the entire matter a thing of the past," she said. "If I happen to see Bill again it will be just impersonal."[17]

Jurges never contacted her, either, and he even refused to talk about the incident with his friends. (He did see her at least one more time, however. Some months later, he, Woody English and a few other Cub players were

Standing in a Chicago courtroom are *(from left to right)*: attorney Herbert G. Immenhausen, Violet Popovich, attorney James M. Burke and ballplayer Billy Jurges. *Associated Press.*

in a North Side bowling alley, and one of them spotted Violet. "We ran out of there like a bullet!" English recalled. "Everybody made a beeline out of that joint!")

Jurges was anxious to play baseball, but just a few days after he and Violet appeared in court, the ballplayer was back in the hospital, complaining of pain in his right side. Much to the doctors' surprise, the discomfort was caused by a bullet lodged between two ribs. Although only two wounds had been found after the shooting, Billy had apparently been shot three times, not twice. Physicians could not rule out the possibility, however, that the bullet that had struck his hand had lodged in his body and been overlooked.

In any case, the surgery proved to be just a minor setback for him, as Billy took the field in Pittsburgh for a July 22 game against the Pirates. In his absence, the usual Cub third baseman, Woody English, had been playing shortstop, and now "the celebrated revolver target" took third base, as he would have less stretching to do there than at his old position.

The Cubs lost, 3–1, though, as a sportswriter observed, "Jurges bowed himself back into his profession by socking a single to center."[18]

If Billy had been reading the newspapers, he would have known that Violet was preparing to resume her own profession as well. On the day the sports pages published Billy's return to the ballpark, she returned to the Chicago stage—but this time singing in a burlesque theater as "The Girl Who Shot for Love."

Violet Popovich was obviously no "shrinking Violet," but self-promotion with a flashy catchphrase could advance her career only so far. Billy had promptly delivered a hit when he stepped up to the plate, but Violet's attempt to jump-start her career by walking onto a burlesque stage would prove to be not nearly so auspicious an occasion.

3

"THE GIRL WHO SHOT FOR LOVE"

She neither looks nor behaves like "the cabaret gun girl."
—Chicago Daily News, *July 27, 1932*

"I'm going to stay home for the time being," Violet Popovich told reporters after Judge John A. Sbarbaro dismissed her court case. She apparently, though, soon grew bored with just her mother for companionship, for she wasted little time in capitalizing on her newfound celebrity status. After their brief road trip to Pittsburgh, Billy Jurges and the Cubs returned to Chicago on July 24 to discover thousands of leaflets distributed around Wrigley Field promoting Popovich's stage performance. Although Jurges had refused to sign a complaint against her, she jumped at the chance to sign a contract to headline in a burlesque show at Chicago's State-Congress Theatre.

The yellow fliers were also strewn around downtown streets. Intrigued passersby who stooped to pick them up read on one side:

Violet Popovich
Under the Stage Name of Violet Valli
In Person at the State-Congress!
The Girl Who Shot for Love

And on the other side:

The Cabaret Gun Girl
Finds Solace in a Return to the Stage
At Chicago's Coolest Theater![19]

A newspaper advertisement promotes both Violet Popovich's performance at Chicago's State-Congress Theatre and her opening burlesque act, featuring the "Bare Cub Girls." *From the* Chicago Herald and Examiner, *July 23, 1932.*

The State-Congress was one of assorted theaters along the southern fringes of Chicago's Loop (the principal business district) that featured burlesque performances. Burlesque entertainment had grown popular in the mid-nineteenth century through skits that ridiculed, or "burlesqued," the social affectations and attitudes of the upper class. Many comedians and actors of the twentieth century honed their skills in early burlesque houses, including Bud Abbott and Lou Costello, W.C. Fields, Jackie Gleason, Al Jolson, Phil Silvers and Red Skelton. Theater owners were always looking for ways to increase attendance, and they began featuring scantily clad showgirls. By the 1920s, striptease acts containing at least partial nudity were common in Chicago's burlesque theaters. In fact, the first nude striptease purportedly took place at the city's State-Congress Theatre in 1928, when Hinda Wassau's costume fell off during a dance. The audience applauded wildly, of course, and Wassau soon went from chorus girl to main attraction.

The State-Congress, at 531 South State Street, was located in an area south of Van Buren Street that was notorious for its disreputable saloons and pool halls, shabby rooming houses and hotels, seedy brothels and dingy burlesque theaters. Theaters survived in Depression-era Chicago "only by exceeding their nearest competitor in salaciousness," contends a burlesque historian. "Chicago particularly abounded in such houses. Respectable women hardly ever ventured into the State-Congress Theatre on the underworld side of State Street. Its formula was simple: 'Shake It Up!'"

There was no shaking going on, however, when a "modestly gowned" Violet stepped out from behind the State-Congress curtain. Performing under her *Vanities* professional name, Violet Valli, she and her "Bare Cub Girls" made their debut on July 23, 1932, in "Bare Cub Follies" (also called "Bare Cub Frolics"). The show was billed as "A Screamingly Funny Burlesque Production," and *Chicago Daily News* drama critic Lloyd Lewis was in the audience when it opened:

> *Some 900 men and boys, coatless and dull-faced, sit staring at the stage. They are mostly lone wolves. There is no gayety in a burlesque theater audience.*
>
> *For an hour they watch the regular burlesque show unfold. It winds its way monotonously through a series of low, boresome sketches by talentless comedians in baggy trousers. There is not much laughter at any moment, and such as there is comes only when the snickering comedians utter words taboo*

Famed American photographer John Vachon captures a burlesque house on South State Street in Chicago. *Library of Congress.*

> *in ordinary society. Between these blackouts, some six young women, one at a time, perform the "stripper" act, which has been standard in burlesque for the last six years. This consists of nothing more complicated than the simple parade of a burlesque lady up and down the runway while the orchestra plays music pretendedly frenzied. The lady who promenades does not sing, she does not dance, except to make certain gauche and awkward imitations of the oldest of oriental contortions. What she does do is to disrobe, bit by bit, in order to keep the audience in favor of encores. Some of the State-Congress "strippers" achieve the dignity of five or six encores, by which time they are fairly nude. Others are allowed to pass with the majority of their garments still upon their backs.*
>
> *The show drones on for almost an hour. Then a smirking and plum tenor in a dinner jacket announces Miss Valli. Curtains in the rear center open and she appears, a tall, brown-haired girl, well dressed, even modestly gowned. Near-nude chorus girls, puffy faced comedians, stage hand*[s] *in undershirts push unabashedly into the wings to stare at her.*
>
> *She neither looks nor behaves like "the cabaret gun girl." She stands nervously while the orchestra rasps off a few bars of a popular love ballad. Then she sings it; not bad, not good; so-so; a quiet little voice. She smiles with the professional showgirl's smile, a nice enough smile. She comes to the end of her song. The patrons expect her to start disrobing like the other prima donnas of the company.*
>
> *She does not. She merely walks off bowing. There are a few scattering handclaps. She takes a bow, then retires without a single gesture of salaciousness.*
>
> *The patrons begin to leave, one man from his row, one man from that. The girl has revealed nothing of her person nor of her adventure with Mr. Jurges of the Chicago National League Baseball Club. She has behaved with more decorous manners, if lesser voice, than many a young woman in legitimate musical comedy—and this is very, very disappointing to the males who have listened to the soiled little handbills screaming from the sidewalks.*[20]

Since Violet revealed neither bare skin nor juicy gossip, it did not take long for the public's curiosity to wear off. "The Girl Who Shot for Love" was supposed to travel the burlesque circuit and perform in theaters around the area, but her show ran for only a few weeks at the State-Congress before quietly closing. Interestingly, a family member would later suggest that her lack of success may have stemmed from her lack of talent. "She liked to sing," her nephew said. "That is, she *tried* to sing."[21]

But Popovich had more important matters to worry about than her floundering stage career. On August 12, she once again appeared before Judge John A. Sbarbaro; this time, she sought his assistance in obtaining a warrant for the arrest of real estate broker Lucius Barnett, her former bail bondsman, on the charge of larceny. She told the judge that while she was in the hospital, she had entrusted Barnett with twenty-five letters from Billy Jurges of, she said, "an affectionate nature." They also purportedly included notes from Kiki Cuyler going back two years. She had asked Barnett to give the correspondence to her attorney, Herbert G. Immenhausen, as she was contemplating suing—for reasons unknown—both ballplayers. She later changed her mind about the lawsuit, but Barnett had refused to return the letters, telling her that he wanted to publish them in booklet form as *The Love Letters of a Shortstop* and sell copies at ballparks around the country. "What do you care about Jurges?" Barnett had brusquely asked her. "We'll drive him out of the Cubs uniform and back to Brooklyn where he belongs."

Barnett had promised her $5,000 up front and $20,000 later, but Popovich declined his offer, saying that she thought too much of Jurges to cooperate in such a plan. The street-smart judge was skeptical of Violet's story, undoubtedly thinking that $25,000 was an outrageous figure for a small book of reprinted letters that few people outside Chicago would be interested in reading. He also sensed some sort of con game that might embarrass his favorite baseball team, commenting, "This looks like a publicity scheme. Besides, I'm a Cub fan myself."

Sbarbaro telephoned Barnett, who told the judge that the letters were his and that he was not returning them. Sbarbaro met with Violet privately in his chambers, telling her that the case was not in his jurisdiction but suggesting that her attorney seek an injunction against Barnett. The judge then addressed reporters, telling them that "publication of letters that would hurt Jurges or the Cubs must be prevented." He added that he had advised Popovich exactly what to do to get the letters returned to her.[22]

The next day, police officers also did their part to help out—among them Pat Roche, the chief investigator for the Illinois state's attorney's office, and his assistant, Sergeant Louis Capparelli. They both had plenty of experience dealing with all matter of criminals. Eliot Ness had not yet formed his "Untouchables" when, in 1927, Roche led a raid on one of Al Capone's biggest breweries, seizing equipment valued at more than $100,000. Capparelli was just as fearless. He and two other police officers had each received the *Chicago Daily Tribune*'s monthly $100 "hero award" after they

Violet Popovich liked sports and enjoyed the company of baseball players. An unidentified young man rests his catching arm on Violet's shoulder. *MA&IJ Prescott Joint Trust.*

shot and killed three kidnappers and extortionists who refused to surrender but instead drew their guns.

Sergeant Capparelli undoubtedly figured that the bespectacled Lucius Barnett would come quietly when he stopped at the bail bondsman's home to pick him up for questioning. And the policeman was right—up to a point. Everything was fine until the two men entered the Metropolitan Building on North LaSalle Street, where Roche had his office. Barnett then saw his opportunity:

> *Barnett kicked Policeman Louis Ca*[p]*parelli of the state's attorney's force and broke away....Policeman Ca*[p]*parelli, although painfully injured, leaped from the floor where he had fallen and seized Barnett on the sidewalk.*
>
> *While they were struggling Policeman David Levine and Julius Siegen, who were waiting with Miss Valli in a restaurant in the building, ran out and joined three traffic policemen, all of whom aided in subduing the man. Pat Roche, who was to have questioned Barnett, had come downstairs by this time and he ordered the prisoner locked up at the detective bureau.*[23]

Judging from Capparelli's hard-nosed manner, Barnett's fate could have been a lot worse. Roche soon discovered Barnett's true motives after talking with Popovich. While the Cubs were in New York in late July and early August playing the Brooklyn Dodgers, he had pressured Violet to telephone Billy. It was Barnett, though, who did all the talking. He threatened to sue the ballplayer if Jurges did not give him $20,000. Barnett ("an alleged confidence man," according to one investigative reporter) had a similar scheme in mind for Kiki Cuyler. His real intention was to blackmail the ballplayers, not publish the letters or file lawsuits.

Violet preferred charges of larceny and extortion, and the police added assault, disorderly conduct and resisting a policeman to the bail bondsman's growing list of offenses. Shortly thereafter, an aggrieved Barnett related his own version of events to a local reporter:

> *I was called in on Miss Valli's case by our pastor* [Jacob Pister] *at the church whose orphanage reared Miss Valli. The pastor asked me to help her out when she got in trouble. I went on her bond and took her to a hospital after she was released for treatment of her gunshot wound. I okayed the bills at the hospital and with the doctors....*

> *I took Miss Valli to her home from the hospital and she took out these letters from the trunk and told me to take them away.*
>
> *Later, Miss Valli decided she wanted the letters back and even came with a policeman one night to get them. I offered to burn them up in her presence as soon as she had paid her hospital bills. She indicated that she had no intention of paying the bills I had indorsed.*[24]

Barnett added that he had been "taking it on the chin by not saying anything in answer to these charges against me." He ominously implied that a scandal was brewing because of the sensual material contained in the letters, which would be devastating to both the Cubs and the National League. Furthermore, he added, "I have it in black and white that Miss Valli has previously embarrassed both Jurges and Kiki Cuyler."

Barnett could produce no evidence about any Popovich-Jurges-Cuyler scandal. Sbarbaro heard the charges against the real estate broker on August 23, listening as Barnett insisted he had not kicked Sergeant Capparelli and that he had tried to flee from the policeman only because he feared he was being kidnapped. The judge, unmoved by Barnett's self-serving arguments, fined him $100 on each of the three police charges.

By now, Barnett had given Violet some, but not all, of her letters, and Judge Sbarbaro scheduled the two remaining charges of larceny and extortion for a September 8 hearing in felony court. Judge Frank M. Padden, however, dismissed the charges for want of prosecution, as litigant Violet Popovich (reportedly sick) failed to appear.

Sergeant Capparelli said in court that he had learned that all of her letters had finally been returned. With the case resolved, Chicago's newspapers quickly turned their attention from the sad saga of Billy and Violet to other matters. One baseball historian later summarized, "After two months of criminalities and sensationalism, the episode had ended with a whimper."[25]

Violet Popovich, however, was not yet finished with making headlines. She once again pursued her show business career, and in 1937 she was on stage singing sentimental love songs in the Kitty Davis Cocktail Lounge on Jackson and Wabash in Chicago. On March 11, her friend Frederick B. Williams, a local businessman who worked in the office of his father's hardware factory, drove to the lounge to pick her up. He became angry at having to wait for her to finish her act and change her clothes, and they started arguing. The fight escalated in his car after she demanded that he take her home, and he began speeding along the streets of Chicago. Ignoring red lights and stop

Two matchbook covers advertising Chicago's Kitty Davis cocktail lounge. In 1937, Violet Popovich performed as a singer in the lounge. *Author's collection.*

signs, he loudly berated her as she demanded that he stop the car. "I insisted he let me out," she told a policeman, "and he said, 'O.K., I'll let you out.' He opened the door and pushed me out."

Popovich suffered minor scrapes and bruises after her hasty and unexpected fall, and the police advised her to file charges against Williams, whom she had been seeing for four years. Hot tempers apparently cooled; on October 13, the two applied for a marriage license, though they never married.

Chicago's newspapers were quick to cover Popovich's automobile altercation, though the reporters did not mention her former fight in the Hotel Carlos—and she certainly was not going to bring it up. Only someone who recognized her would have made the connection. Following Violet's divorce, she sometimes used her mother's birth name (which Margaret Popovich assumed after her own divorce in 1920), and the articles focused on one "Violet Heindl" being pushed from the car, not Violet Popovich or Violet Valli.

Violet's name—whether it was Popovich, Valli or Heindl—rarely again made the papers. Sportswriters occasionally wrote pieces on Jurges's career and mentioned the shooting, and columns featuring "this day in history" events sometimes noted it. When a female fan shot Philadelphia Phillies ballplayer (and ex-Cub) Eddie Waitkus in his Chicago hotel room in 1949, Jurges and Popovich emerged as a casual footnote in some of the news articles.[26]

These brief stories provided no new details about Violet, though, truth be told, relatively little about her was published after the shooting anyway. Who were her parents? What was her childhood like? Few people outside her family seemed to have known much about her, but a close examination of her formative years provides insights into what may have led to her decision to confront Billy Jurges in his hotel room on July 6, 1932, and swiftly pull a gun from her purse.

4

VIOLET'S TROUBLED PAST

After the baby was born he hit me in the face and over the body, and he gave me black and blue eyes.
—From the March 1920 divorce hearing of Margaret Popovich

Mirko Popovic was twenty-five years old when he stepped off the ship in New York City on January 19, 1907. Born in Austria, Popovic had black hair and brown eyes and was five feet, eight inches tall. He had sailed from Hamburg, Germany, aboard the SS *Kaiserin Auguste Victoria*. After hours of being fogbound in New York Harbor, the Hamburg-American liner had finally managed to dock.

Popovic, an electrician by trade, soon settled in Chicago, and in 1910, he married Margaret Heindl, age nineteen, also from Austria. The couple had their first child, Viola, on March 21, 1911. Four other children would join their big sister: Drogiro (a girl born in 1912 but surviving only a few weeks), Michael in 1913, Milos in 1915 and Marco in 1917.[27]

After a few years in the United States, Mirko Popovic Americanized his name to Michael (also Mike) Popovich, Viola became Violet, and Marco would soon answer to Mark. Both Mark and his brother Mike would eventually change their last names to Prescott. Milos would later change his name to Melvin Parker and then to Melvin Parker Popovich.[28]

The Popovich marriage was not a happy one. As recorded in court documents, Margaret lived "in constant fear" of her husband, and he began beating her soon after Violet's birth. "At that time my baby was only ten days old," Margaret testified at a March 11, 1920 divorce hearing. "After the baby was born he hit me in the face and over the body, and he gave me black and blue eyes." To bolster the case of the battered woman, her attorney even put eight-year-old Violet on the stand, though she was asked only a few perfunctory questions:

Q: What is your name?
A: Violet Popovich.
Q: The complainant is your mother?
A: Yes.
Q: How old are you?
A: I will be nine years in March.
Q: Do you understand the meaning of an oath?
A: No.
Q: When you raise your hand do you understand what you are doing?
A: No.
Q: Do you go to Sunday school?
A: No.
Q: Do you know what would happen to you if you did not tell the truth?
A: Yes, I would be put in jail.[29]

In the divorce decree, dated March 30, 1920, the court stated that Michael Popovich had been guilty of "extreme and repeated cruelty" toward Margaret. The court ordered him to pay his ex-wife "as alimony for the support of herself and children the sum of fifteen dollars each and every week." Popovich worked as a night electrician in Chicago's Insurance Exchange Building, but despite his comfortable salary, he repeatedly ignored both the court's order and his family's poverty.

Margaret petitioned Chicago's circuit court in late July, declaring that Michael had not paid any alimony since their divorce and that he owed her $250. Margaret did not earn enough as a seamstress in a dressmaking establishment to provide for herself and her four children and desperately needed her ex-husband's financial assistance. Her petition noted that she was "unable to support the said children which she was given custody of, in a sanitary and wholesome manner and without the aid of the said alimony, [she] would be compelled to bring up the said ch[i]ldren in poor surroundings."[30]

The youngsters consequently were sent to Chicago's Uhlich Evangelical Lutheran Orphan Asylum, later known as the Uhlich Children's Home. A

The Boys' Band of the Uhlich Children's Home. The words "Orphan Home" are carved above the door. *MA&LJ Prescott Joint Trust.*

private institution on the corner of Burling Street and Center Street (now Armitage Avenue) and relocated in 1928 to 3730 North California Avenue, the Uhlich home cared for children without parents or whose parents could not provide for them. It was founded in 1867 as part of the German St. Paul's Evangelical and Reformed Church in Chicago (later called St. Paul's United Church of Christ). Violet even sang in the church choir of St. Paul's, a handsome structure at the corner of Orchard Street and Kemper Place. She was well known in the parish, with one member observing that she was "a fine young church-going girl."

The court ordered Michael Popovich to pay for his children's room and board at the orphanage, though he did so only begrudgingly. The home's superintendent told the Uhlich board of trustees in April 1928 that "after we had him in the Court of Domestic Relations," Popovich paid $200 toward his bill, but he was still in arrears more than $300. By June, the debt had finally been settled.

The Popovich boys were residents until 1932; in fact, in 1928, Mike told the superintendent that the orphanage was the only real home he had

Left: After their parents divorced, the four Popovich children lived for years at the Uhlich Children's Home. Standing by the orphanage is Violet, the eldest. *MA&LJ Prescott Joint Trust.*

Right: Violet Popovich's three younger brothers pose outside the Uhlich Children's Home. *From left to right*: Michael, Milos (later Melvin) and Mark. *MA&LJ Prescott Joint Trust.*

ever known. Violet, however, hated foster care and wanted to live with her mother. She got her wish in 1922, after she deliberately started a fire in one of Uhlich's bathrooms. Violet's mother evidently could not care for (or perhaps could not control) her daughter, for the girl wound up back in the orphanage.

Violet still preferred her mother over a matron, and in early 1926, shortly before her fifteenth birthday, she told the Uhlich administrators that she would soon turn eighteen and asked for permission to leave. Her request was granted (apparently without verification of her true age), though four months later the girl probably regretted her decision. The *Chicago Daily Tribune* reported that the local police were called when the fifteen-year-old ran away from her mother's house after being "whipped for going to a movie with a boy and staying out late."[31]

With such a childhood, it is hardly surprising that Violet married just three years later—and was divorced soon afterward. The lonely and unhappy teenager undoubtedly saw the stage as a glamorous alternative to her dismal home life, for after taking dance classes she got a temporary job in a Chicago production of *Earl Carroll Vanities*. Theatrical producer Earl Carroll's popular series of musical revues featured, in his words, "the most beautiful girls in the world," and Violet was immediately captivated by the elaborate sets and lavish production numbers.

Carroll produced his *Vanities* in series he called "editions." The seventh edition, which originally opened in New York in 1928, played in January and February 1930 at the Erlanger Theatre on 127 North Clark Street, located in the heart of the city's Loop. Since this show was the only "edition" performed in Chicago in 1930, it seems likely that it marked Violet's first professional appearance before the footlights.

The seventh edition of *Vanities* included forty-seven brief skits, musical numbers and dance performances, which, as described by a reviewer, "succeed each other with almost bewildering speed, accompanied by miraculous scene shifting." Comedian W.C. Fields was the headline attraction. In a sketch that he wrote, "The Caledonian Express," he played in turn a train guard, a stationmaster, a conductor and a policeman—all summoned to settle a dispute between passengers as to who had the right to stay in a train compartment.

The theater company numbered one hundred people, including fifty-six chorus girls. Newspapers reported after the shooting that Popovich had sung in the chorus of the Chicago *Vanities*, so one of her acts must have been "I'm Flyin' High," a musical routine in which the chorus members formed the shape of an airplane, complete with a cartwheeling young woman who simulated the plane's propeller. The show concluded with the chorus waving goodbye to the theater audience through a curtain of ostrich plumes.[32]

Violet's pursuit of a theatrical career stemmed from her longtime friendship with an actress who was quite at home on the stage. This woman, as it turned out, was in all likelihood her confidante (and confederate) in her showdown with Billy Jurges at the Hotel Carlos. In its coverage of the shooting, one Chicago newspaper related that as Violet stood before the door of his hotel room, a "mysterious girl friend" with her "turned and fled." Another paper put some of the pieces together when it wrote that on the night before the shooting, Violet and her "girl chum, known as 'Betty,'" had engaged in target practice in an alley in back of the hotel. A

Violet Popovich performed in *Earl Carroll Vanities* in early 1930. This advertisement promotes the ninth edition, or series, of the musical revue, produced in 1931. *Author's collection.*

third mentioned that the police were looking for Violet's "mysterious blond companion," adding that Violet's mother knew her as "Betty."[33]

Margaret Heindl no doubt could have revealed more than just a first name, as the mystery woman was likely Violet's stepsister, Betty Subject (original name Sopcak). In 1922, Michael Popovich had married Anna Sopcak, a janitor in the same building where he worked, when her daughter Betty was twenty-six and Violet, eleven. By then, Betty had earned favorable reviews as an accomplished theater actress, particularly for her performance in the 1914 musical comedy *September Morn.*

Betty and Violet had something in common: they were both quite familiar with the abusive Michael Popovich. Shortly after Anna and Michael's marriage, she gave him $6,200—an inheritance from her first husband—to purchase a three-story brick and stone apartment building containing six flats at 538–540 Belden Street in Chicago. Unbeknownst to her, however, title was taken in both their names. In 1929, she successfully sued to have the title to the property reformed so that she was the sole owner. During the lengthy proceeding, which lasted many months, Betty testified that she had once had her stepfather arrested after he attacked and beat her mother. Betty also testified in her mother's 1930 divorce hearing that "he kicked my mother in the side and struck her and when I said, 'How dare you strike her,' he kicked me three times."[34]

Right: An attractively dressed Violet Popovich stands on a Chicago street corner. *MA&LJ Prescott Joint Trust.*

Below: Violet Popovich (*top*). The unidentified woman sitting below her resembles (and possibly is) stage actress Betty Subject, Violet's stepsister. *MA&LJ Prescott Joint Trust.*

But Betty had her own share of problems. After she filed for divorce in 1923 from her second husband, music arranger Harold A. Powell (she would marry twice more), newspapers reported on the seamy details of her personal life. One paper noted that Powell, an elder in the Methodist Church, "frequently became intoxicated, and associated with other women." When she could not pay her rent in early 1924, another newspaper unsympathetically proclaimed, "September Morn out of Luck." Violet paid little attention to such articles, however, for she looked up to her stepsister as a true "big sister." When Violet sought employment on the New York stage in May 1932, it was only natural that Betty accompanied her.

Violet needed a trusted confidante, so it was logical that when she made plans to see Billy Jurges in the Hotel Carlos two months later, Betty was nearby to provide moral support. But did Betty urge Violet to put a pistol in her purse before walking upstairs to his room? Was it Betty's idea to go target shooting behind the hotel? A Chicago historian well familiar with the family history commented that "Betty was the troublemaker and I think it was Betty who led Violet astray."

Nothing is known about the two women's relationship following Violet's reckless confrontation with Billy, except that they both settled in Los Angeles, California. Little information is available about Betty, either. Her fourth husband, Eugene S. Carlan, died in 1945, and she passed away with scant notice in Los Angeles in 1970. She left a sister, Evelyn Subject, born in 1893, and a son, Harold A. Powell Jr., born in 1916.

Violet did not tell the police all the details behind the shooting, and it is unfortunate that officers could not locate Violet's "mysterious blond companion." As the featured co-conspirator in the Hotel Carlos gunplay, Betty certainly could have answered most—if not all—of their questions.[35]

5

JUST "ONE THING AFTER ANOTHER" FOR THE CUBS

Aside from the pitching, the excellent work of Johnny Moore in the outfield, and the fielding of [Billy] *Jurges in the early part of the year, until he was shot by an admirer in an affair of the heart, were the principal reasons for the team's early showing.*
—Chicago Daily Tribune, *September 21, 1932*

Chewing-gum magnate William Wrigley Jr. had initially viewed the Cubs merely as an investment when he and other financial backers purchased the team from Charles P. Taft—the half brother of U.S. president William Howard Taft—in 1916. But Wrigley's interest in the club gradually grew, and by January 1919, he had become not only its major stockholder but also an enthusiastic, devoted fan.

It was difficult, however, for baseball fans to generate much enthusiasm for the team when the players displayed so little of it themselves. "The Cubs drifted aimlessly through the early part of the 1920s," a sportswriter observed, "and thudded into last place in 1925 under three different managers." Following that disastrous season, Wrigley hired as his manager Joe McCarthy, who had led the minor-league Louisville Colonels to the American Association championship that year. It was a shrewd move; by 1928, the Cubs had climbed to third place in the National League.[36]

After the Cubs acquired slugger Rogers Hornsby from the Boston Braves in November, many journalists predicted that Chicago would easily win the 1929 National League pennant. Ample evidence supported

In this 1929 photograph, Chicago Cub manager Joe McCarthy (*left*) talks with team owner William Wrigley Jr. and President William Veeck. *Author's collection.*

them, for just a few weeks earlier, Hornsby had clinched his seventh NL batting title. As one of baseball's premier hitters, he had also led the league in batting from 1920 to 1925, and in 1925, he had taken home the league's Most Valuable Player Award. "The addition of Rogers Hornsby to an already imposing list of hitters is the reason for the heavy vote cast for the Cubs," one sportswriter acknowledged that April. The Cubs did indeed win the 1929 pennant with a 98-54-4 record, ten and a half games in front of the second-place Pittsburgh Pirates, with Hornsby batting .380 for the season, leading the league with 156 runs scored and once again winning the MVP Award.

But the Philadelphia Athletics, managed by the renowned Cornelius McGillicuddy, better known as Connie Mack, were also steamrolling teams over in the American League, and the Athletics ended the season with a 104-46-1 record, a full eighteen games ahead of the second-place New York Yankees. The Athletics carried that momentum into the World Series, and much to the bitter disappointment of William Wrigley, they decisively trounced Chicago in October, four games to one.[37]

Chicago Cubs manager Joe McCarthy, photographed shortly after the start of the 1930 season. He would be fired five months later. *Library of Congress.*

By the spring of 1930, Wrigley was predicting another pennant, as he believed his team was "20 per cent stronger than in 1929." On August 27, the Cubs held a comfortable five-and-a-half-game lead, but then the losses began piling up. This did not bode well for McCarthy, as close observers believed that Wrigley blamed him for the humiliating World Series loss the year before. The Cubs were two and a half games out of first place on September 22, and Wrigley had had enough; that evening, he announced that McCarthy would not be managing the team in 1931 and that Cubs infielder Rogers Hornsby would be the new player-manager:

> *I realize that Joe McCarthy is one of baseball's greatest managers, but I must have a winner. I have always wanted a world's championship team and I'm not so sure that McCarthy is the man to give me that kind of a team. I was sadly disappointed after the world series of last year. I believe we should have won....I have my mind set on having the greatest team in either league in the next year or so, and to do so I must have a manager who can pilot it into that position. I believe Hornsby is the man."*[38]

Chicago Cubs owner William Wrigley Jr. watches his team play on a cold April day in 1930. *Library of Congress.*

Wrigley's belief undoubtedly stemmed from Hornsby's impressive baseball credentials, though the player's abilities on the field were overshadowed by his notoriously acerbic disposition and utter lack of diplomacy. Wrigley admitted that "the move may not be popular with the fans," and it certainly did not meet the approval of Cubs president William L. Veeck Sr. Veeck, a shrewd and well-respected baseball man who for many years had contributed a sports column to the *Chicago Evening American*. In December 1918, the Cubs' board of directors had elected him vice president and treasurer, and he assumed the president's position the following July. According to Veeck's son Bill, the only argument his father and William Wrigley ever had arose over the hiring of Hornsby as manager. The Cubs' president was dead set against the decision, particularly as Wrigley made it "over my father's head."[39]

Wrigley should have listened to Veeck. McCarthy did not wait for the season to end but resigned and joined the New York Yankees as manager, while Hornsby quickly assumed direction of the Cubs. Chicago finished in second place in 1930 and fell to third in 1931, seventeen games behind the St. Louis Cardinals. By 1932, though, the Cubs rebounded and by midseason were still in the pennant chase. On the morning Violet shot Billy, Chicago was only three games behind league-leading Pittsburgh. The Cubs kept battling, but after their loss to Pittsburgh on July 22—the day Jurges rejoined his teammates—they found themselves three and a half games behind the Pirates.

Although little had changed on the field while Jurges was out of the lineup, there was plenty going on behind the scenes. Whispered comments within the Cubs' organization centered on the obvious animosity between club president William Veeck Sr. and manager Rogers Hornsby. Veeck believed that the team was easily good enough to win the National League pennant, and he was growing weary of Hornsby's constant carping about the men and their alleged shortcomings.

Veeck also disagreed with Hornsby's managerial style. For example, he had told Hornsby that Chicago should have won the game against Pittsburgh on July 22. Why had the manager not called a clubhouse meeting beforehand

Three stars of the 1930 Chicago Cubs (*left to right*): center fielder Hack Wilson, second baseman Rogers Hornsby and right fielder Kiki Cuyler. *Library of Congress.*

to discuss strategy? Hornsby replied that the Cubs had already played the Pirates that year and he did not think a meeting was necessary. He added that if Veeck did not like the way he managed the team, then he would step aside and Veeck could hire someone else.

As *The Sporting News* aptly put it, "After that it was as plain as the nose on your face that the temperature between them had dropped to freezing." And it certainly was just as frigid between Hornsby and his players. They had little use for their brusque and no-nonsense manager, who publicly (and frequently) pointed out their mistakes while rebuking the players for not measuring up to his unrealistic standards. "He was a very cold man," second baseman Billy Herman recalled years later. "He would stare at you with the coldest eyes I ever saw. If you did something wrong, he'd jump all over you. He was a perfectionist and had a very low tolerance for mistakes. He was one of the greatest hitters that ever lived—maybe the greatest—but he never talked hitting with us. He just expected you to go up there and do it."[40]

Hornsby's surliness and inflexible nature were bad enough, but a major—and embarrassing—scandal involving the manager and some of the players soon made news around the country. A loss to the Brooklyn Dodgers on August 2 put the Cubs five games behind the first-place Pittsburgh Pirates. That evening, team president William Veeck fired Hornsby and appointed as manager the popular first baseman and team captain, Charlie "Jolly Cholly" Grimm (who named veteran Woody English as the new captain). The team members were relieved that Hornsby was gone, but the manager's firing worried a few players; Hornsby owed them money, and they wanted to be repaid! It turned out that Hornsby was an inveterate better on racehorses, and to cover his gambling debts over the previous few years he had borrowed thousands of dollars from infielder Woody English, coach Charley O'Leary and pitchers Guy Bush, Pat Malone and Bob Smith.

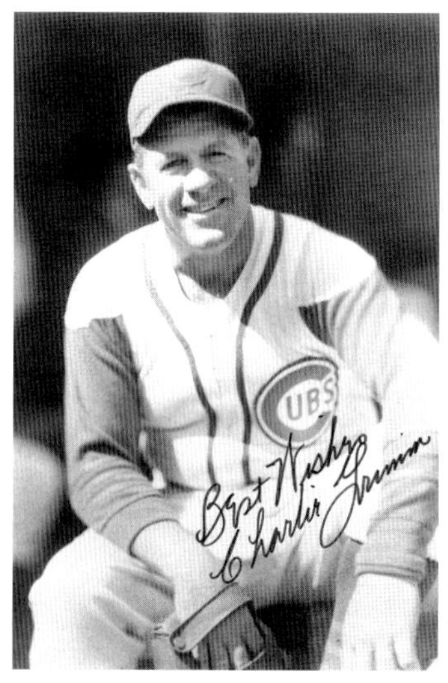

The affable Charlie Grimm managed the Chicago Cubs to National League pennants in 1932, 1935 and 1945. *Author's collection.*

Veeck admitted that he had fired Hornsby the day he first learned of the loans but insisted that he had made up his mind to let

Hornsby go days before then. "We made a change in managers…for only one reason—to increase our chances of winning a pennant for Chicago," Veeck said firmly. "We felt we couldn't do it with Rogers Hornsby and believed we could do it with Charl[ie] Grimm….If [Hornsby] gambled on the horses I know nothing of it." Grimm was of a similar mind. Although he felt that Hornsby and Veeck were "like the irresistible force colliding with an immovable object," he thought that the gambling charges had "little or nothing" to do with Veeck's decision.

Some of the city's newspapers saw things differently, particularly the *Chicago Daily News*, which on August 11 reported on a "sweeping inquiry into charges of horse-race gambling by players" during Hornsby's term as manager. Veeck was furious, and that evening he released a statement declaring that the feature story about the Cub players gambling was "one of the most outrageous incidents in baseball history" and "a cheap, cowardly attack." Nevertheless, it all had to be checked out thoroughly, and the man for the job was the autocratic commissioner of baseball, Kenesaw Mountain Landis. Landis, a former judge, had built an imposing reputation and had helped to restore the American public's faith in organized baseball following the infamous 1919 "Black Sox" scandal.

Landis launched an investigation into the Cubs and the gambling charges, and Hornsby, English, Bush, Malone and O'Leary testified before him in a special hearing on August 13, the details of which were well publicized in newspapers. The married Bush was especially upset, as the papers also reported he was often seen with two blond women who supposedly worked for a local bookmaker. "I think that story is terrible, judge," Bush protested. "I don't give a damn what anybody says, it is lousy." After Landis listened to the evidence, he agreed with him. Bush and his teammates were cleared of all charges, as the testimonies revealed that only Hornsby had gambled on horse races. Hornsby testified that he had borrowed $11,350 from the men through loans or the endorsement of notes, which he used, he said rather incredulously, to pay taxes and the mortgage interest on his home. A total of $6,175 had been paid back, and Hornsby produced a signed agreement with club president William Veeck as to how the rest of the money would be repaid.[41]

It is difficult to believe that Veeck had not been aware of Hornsby's gambling and his borrowing of money from the ballplayers. The press thought Veeck knew the details; furthermore, Hornsby was so disliked by his players that Veeck must have heard the player grumblings, which undoubtedly hurt team morale.

Left: During his twenty-four-year tenure as baseball's first commissioner (1920–44), Kenesaw Mountain Landis ruled the sport with an iron hand. *Author's collection.*

Below: Chicago Cubs owner Philip K. Wrigley and his wife, Helen, attend a game at Wrigley Field. *Author's collection.*

Perhaps also affecting team morale was the change in the club's ownership. Following a stroke and a heart attack, popular William Wrigley—for whom the Cubs' ballpark, Wrigley Field, was named in 1926—had died on January 26, 1932, at age seventy, leaving his son, Philip Knight "P.K." Wrigley, in charge of the family chewing-gum company and the Chicago Cubs. The younger Wrigley, unfortunately, was not particularly interested in baseball in general or the Cubs in particular. "Anything Veeck does is all right with me," he had told reporters soon after the club president dismissed Hornsby as manager. "I don't know much about baseball. It's Veeck's job to see that the Cubs win a pennant."[42]

And since the Landis hearing had exonerated the players, Veeck could now turn his full attention to winning the pennant. He had been concerned about Billy Jurges's recovery following the shooting, and just a few days after Philip K. Wrigley talked to the press, the club president announced that he had acquired ballplayer Mark Koenig to help out in the infield. Koenig had joined the New York Yankees in 1925 and in 1930 was traded to the Detroit Tigers. He then batted .335 in eighty-nine games for San Francisco's minor-league Mission Reds before Veeck purchased him for the Cubs. Koenig proved to be an excellent choice, for, as one Chicago sportswriter declared, on August 14 he "hit the first ball thrown to him in the National League for a single, and he has been busting 'em ever since."[43]

The Cubs were also "busting 'em," thanks to new manager Charlie Grimm. "Jolly Cholly" was living up to his nickname; the team flourished under his buoyant personality and easygoing, even-tempered leadership style. "He just let everybody go their way," remembered Billy Herman, "no rules, no curfew. He ran the game on the field, of course, but away from it he was just a happy-go-lucky guy." Both Jurges and Koenig played shortstop for Grimm, though Koenig was making headlines—and heads turn. On August 20 in a game against the Philadelphia Phillies, he became "Chicago's baseball hero of heroes," as one local sportswriter claimed. With two men on base and two out in the ninth inning and the Cubs down, 5–3, Koenig drove Ray Benge's first pitch "high into the right field stands for the wildest of the wild finishes that are becoming habitual with the Cubs."

That wild day marked the first victory in a fourteen-game winning streak that gave the Cubs a solid grip on first place. They clinched the National League pennant on September 20, finishing the season with a record of 90-64, four games in front of the Pittsburgh Pirates. "Never before was a team beset with more irritating experiences apart from the playing of baseball," marveled the *Chicago Daily Tribune*. The newspaper particularly mentioned that despite the well-publicized dismissal of manager Rogers Hornsby, the shooting of star shortstop Billy Jurges and the *Chicago Daily News*' unfounded charges of horse-race gambling, the Cubs managed to battle through them all and prevail. The *Tribune* sportswriter attributed much of their success to outstanding pitching, the batting of outfielder Johnny Moore and "the fielding of [Billy] Jurges in the early part of the year, until he was shot by an admirer in an affair of the heart." Later in the season, the article continued, the hitting and fielding of Mark Koenig "supplied the team with the punch it needed."

Koenig's play did indeed prove to be a key factor in Chicago's drive to the flag, for in his thirty-three games he batted .353. "The ball started bouncing for us the first day Mark put on a Cub uniform," Charlie Grimm recalled years later. Team captain Woody English agreed: "Koenig really helped us."[44]

Some of Koenig's Cub teammates, however, preferred to focus not on his performance but on the relatively few games he had played. They met to vote on the division of the World Series bonuses, as a player's full share required unanimous approval. (Members of the winning team would later each receive $5,231.77, while the losers would get $4,244.60.) Billy Jurges and second baseman Billy Herman insisted that Koenig deserved only a half share, not a full one. "We figured he wasn't entitled to it," Jurges argued. "He did win the pennant for us, but he didn't play that many ball games."

The New York Yankees, Koenig's former team and Chicago's World Series opponents, did not see it that way. When the newspapers announced the breakdown of the World Series money, the Yankees (and Babe Ruth especially) blasted the Cubs as cheapskates and penny-pinchers. "Sure, I'm on 'em," Ruth admitted scornfully in an interview. "I hope we beat 'em four straight. They gave Koenig…a sour deal in [his] player cut. They're chiselers and I tell 'em so."[45]

The Cubs might have had a good chance in the World Series if the Yankees had summarily dismissed them and gone into the games carefree and cocky. Instead, as well-known sportswriter Shirley Povich succinctly appraised the championship showdown, "The Cubs' stinginess fired the Yankees to new heights." The Cubs lost the first two games in New York, 12–6 and 5–2. On October 1, the World Series shifted to Chicago, where 49,986 spectators crammed into Wrigley Field and onto temporary wood bleachers constructed outside the park. The wind was blowing out to right field, and Babe Ruth and Lou Gehrig took turns slamming balls into the stands during batting practice (Ruth belted nine and Gehrig seven). "I'd play for half my salary," Ruth shouted at the Cubs, "if I could hit in this dump all the time."

Chicago Cub third baseman Woody English maintained that Babe Ruth never pointed to center field before hitting a home run during the 1932 World Series. *Author's collection.*

New York took an early lead, thanks to home runs by Ruth and Gehrig, but in the fourth inning, Billy Jurges hit a double and then scored the tying run, making it 4–4. The Chicago crowd was screaming encouragement at the Cubs and abuse at the Yankees, and both teams continued shouting invectives at each other, as they had since the series started. The Cubs, for their part, were particularly vicious toward Ruth, yelling obscenities at him. In the fifth inning, Ruth was at the plate facing pitcher Charlie Root, with the count at two balls and two strikes. The Babe, who was left-handed, then raised his right hand. Did Ruth gesture in derision to the Cubs in the third-base dugout or to Root on the mound—or did he point to center field as if to signal that he was going to hit a home run? Decades later, Cub captain Woody English looked back on the dramatic moment:

> *I was playing third base. I was right close to it. He's got two strikes on him. The guys are yelling at him from our dugout. He's looking right in our dugout, and he holds up two fingers. He said, "That's only two strikes." But the press box was way back on top of Wrigley Field, and to the people in the press, it looked like he pointed to center field. But he was looking right into our dugout and holding two fingers up. That* is *the true story. I've been asked that question five hundred times.*[46]

English added that pitcher Charlie Root "threw hard, had a good curve ball," and when he was on the baseball field "was a competitor all the way." Root himself said that if Ruth had tried to show him up by signaling where he was going to hit the baseball, "Anybody who knows me knows that Ruth would have ended up on his ass."

Others had different opinions, but what happened next is unarguable: Ruth smashed Root's next pitch into the center-field bleachers. Gehrig followed Ruth to the plate and also hit a home run, leaving the Chicago team thoroughly demoralized. "The Yankees just had too much power for us," English sighed. "It was discouraging." The Cubs lost the game, 7–5, and also the next one, 13–6, suffering a four-game sweep, just as Ruth had hoped.

In the dozens of press reports dashed off by on-site reporters that day, only one—written by Joe Williams of the *New York World-Telegram* and titled "Ruth Calls Shot as He Puts Homer No. 2 in Side Pocket"—suggested that Ruth had pointed to center field to "call" or indicate the location of his home-run ball. Some sportswriters mentioned gestures to the dugout rather than the outfield. Others included references to Ruth raising his finger or fingers, but only to signal the pitch count. Many reporters did not mention any gesturing at all but simply described his home run.[47]

Spectators' comments were just as varied as the ones by sportswriters and did not fall along partisan lines. One of Ruth's principal hecklers was Cub pitcher Guy Bush, who was sitting in the Cubs' dugout during the game. "I thought he pointed to the right-center or centerfield bleachers....I believe Ruth meant to call the home run." Pat Pieper announced lineups at Cub games for more than fifty years. He was an eyewitness to the home run and never doubted that Ruth "definitely pointed toward center field." Cub manager Charlie Grimm was playing first base that day. Two months after the World Series, he remarked, "And that Ruth. Calling his shot and hitting one over the center fence." Grimm later reversed himself and declared that "the Babe actually was pointing to the mound." His fellow infielder, shortstop Billy Jurges, disagreed and said that Ruth "pointed to the dugout....The Cubs ballplayers were riding Ruth, and he said, 'Well, that's only two strikes.' Gabby Hartnett, our catcher, heard him."

The Yankees themselves were also of little help. Although some of the New Yorkers (including Gehrig, Lefty Gomez, George Pipgras and Joe Sewell) steadfastly maintained that Ruth pointed to the outfield, others (including Frankie Crosetti, Bill Dickey and manager Joe McCarthy) insisted he did not. Dickey, in fact, admitted to veteran Washington, D.C. sports columnist Shirley Povich that Ruth told his fellow teammates that he did not point to the center-field stands, but for years they all kept quiet. "All of us players could see it was a helluva good story," said Dickey. "So we just made an agreement not to bother straightening out the facts." Ruth himself confessed to baseball trainer Ed Froelich in 1938 that "I may be dumb, but I'm not that dumb. I'm going to point to the center-field bleachers with a barracuda like Root out there? On the next pitch they'd be picking [the ball] out of my ear with a pair of tweezers."[48]

New York Yankee Babe Ruth in 1933. Baseball fans hotly debate whether Ruth "called" his home run in the 1932 Cubs-Yankees World Series. *Wikimedia Commons.*

Instead of "straightening out the facts," however, Ruth enjoyed being the center of attention, and he related assorted versions of his "Called Shot" over the years. Of course, the "Bambino" predicting a home run was not an unusual circumstance. Leigh Montville points out in *The Big Bam: The Life and Times of Babe Ruth*, that "he called shots all the time. He loved to create situations. It was for other people to determine what they meant. Did he call a shot here? That probably never will be answered to every nitpicker's satisfaction."

But does it really matter? Babe Ruth's bat and extraordinary power, as well as his charismatic presence and celebrity status, helped fill ballparks across the country with cheering fans. Whatever took place at Wrigley Field on October 1, 1932, only the "Sultan of Swat" could have flamboyantly transformed a few minutes of baseball into the stuff of American legend. After all, admitted Cub Charlie Grimm years later, "A great guy hit that homer, the greatest slugger of all time." Some of the sportswriters covering the game also picked up on the significance of the moment. The *New York Times* reporter noticed that the Chicago spectators, who had been jeering Ruth just moments before he stepped to the plate, suddenly realized after the ball went sailing overhead that they "had just witnessed an epic feat," and they "hailed the Babe with a salvo of applause" as he exuberantly rounded the bases. Little wonder that Gehrig's subsequent home run is today largely forgotten.

As for unfortunate Charlie Root, the quick-tempered Cub pitcher always denied that the Yankee slugger gestured to center field. When Root was offered a substantial fee to play himself in the movie *The Babe Ruth Story* (1948), he refused, saying, "Not if you're going to show him pointing." Root's resolute feelings on the matter never wavered, and anyone who dared poke fun at him about Ruth's gesture never did so twice. For example, during spring training one year, as Root was pitching during batting practice, a young player defiantly raised his bat toward center field. Root knocked him flat on the ground with his first pitch and proceeded to keep him there as he threw ball after ball at him. "OK, he didn't point!" the player finally shouted. Even Root's family members did not get a free pass. One afternoon, as they all played Wiffle ball during a get-together, Charlie Jr.'s wife made the mistake of pointing her toy bat out to center. Root immediately sent the plastic ball whizzing straight toward his daughter-in-law, hitting her neck.

Root played with the Cubs from 1926 to 1941 and remains the winningest pitcher in club history, holding the franchise record for games played (605), career wins (201) and seasons played (16). For him, however, all that was overshadowed by Game Three of the 1932 World Series. "I gave my whole life to baseball," he said with resignation, "and I'll be remembered for something that never happened."

Whether it happened or not will be debated for as long as fans enjoy a good game of baseball. Chicago Cubs historian and writer Art Ahrens tells the story that his father was sitting on the third-base side of Wrigley Field's grandstand when Ruth hit his home run. The older Ahrens always said that from his angle it looked like Ruth pointed to center field. On the other hand, the writer knew a Catholic priest who was also at the game, sitting along the first-base side, and he always maintained that Ruth was gesturing to the Cubs' dugout. Which one should he believe, the younger Ahrens wonders, his father or the priest?[49]

BILLY JURGES DID HIS part at the plate in the 1932 World Series, batting 4-for-11 in the last three games (.364). During the regular season, he also managed to raise his batting average from the previous year's .201 to .253. In addition, the *Tribune* reported that "Bullet Bill Jurges, though he had many things to distract him," led National League shortstops with his .964 fielding percentage in 108 games (shortstop Dick Bartell of the Phillies played in 154 games and finished the year with a .963 percentage).

Billy Jurges and his bride, the former Mary Elizabeth Reinhart Huyett, after their wedding on June 28, 1933, in Reading, Pennsylvania. *Author's collection.*

Mark Koenig injured his wrist sliding into third base during the first game of the World Series. He managed to pinch-hit in the third game but batted just 1-for-4 in the Fall Classic (.250). He was not surprised at his team's lack of success in the series. "I never fit in with the Cubs players," he said. "They only voted me a half-share of the World Series [money]....I knew damned well we couldn't beat [the Yankees]." Koenig played one more year for the Cubs before he was traded to the Philadelphia Phillies in November 1933.[50]

Baseball journalists and fans at the time protested what they felt was the Cubs' shameful treatment of Koenig. Commissioner Landis even asked team captain Woody English to meet with him to discuss the Koenig vote (Landis agreed with the Cubs). One cannot say, of course, that the Chicago players would have made it to the World Series without Koenig, nor that the Cubs could have defeated a less impassioned Yankee team.

But Chicago still had a lot to be proud of. One reporter concluded that the National League's 1932 season "never will be equaled from the point of view of the Chicago fan." Most journalists had given the Cubs little chance of securing the pennant, but even after being five games out of first place in early August, they managed to claw back and take home the coveted prize. It was just "one thing after another," the reporter said, and "all these things make 1932 to be long remembered by all Cub fans who can make themselves forget that the New York Yankees steam rollered [*sic*] them in the world series in four straight games."[51]

Although Billy Jurges remarked after Violet Popovich shot him that he had no intention of getting married and that "I guess I'll remain a bachelor all my life," he soon changed his mind. On the morning of June 28, 1933, in Reading, Pennsylvania, he married Mary Elizabeth Reinhart Huyett of nearby Birdsboro. One sportswriter felt that she must have provided him with "inspiration," as later on that day he celebrated his nuptials with six hits, including a home run, in a Cubs-Phillies doubleheader (Chicago won both games, 9–5 and 8–3).

He could not have topped off his wedding day in any better fashion.[52]

6

PLAYING HARD AND PLAYING TO WIN

Billy Jurges would go out, play hard, go through a brick wall for you.
—Chicago Cub first baseman Phil Cavarretta

The Cubs continued to enjoy playing baseball for manager Charlie Grimm. His formula of working hard on the field but keeping the mood lighthearted off it seemed to resonate with the players; they finished the 1933 season with a record of eighty-six wins and sixty-eight losses, placing third among the eight teams in the National League. They again finished third in 1934, though that year Billy Jurges saw fewer opportunities than usual to play ball. In early May, he suffered an attack of appendicitis and underwent an operation on June 28, which kept him out of the starting lineup until mid-August. The surgery had a bright side, however; his daughter, Suzanne, was born on April 23, and he enjoyed being a stay-at-home father for a few months.[53]

Despite the relaxed, laid-back atmosphere around the clubhouse, the players did not have to look far to see evidence of the economic hardships brought on by the crippling Great Depression. Unemployment rates across the country soared past 20 percent. In Chicago, half the city's labor force could not find jobs, and countless persons were not working full time. "A man can't go to a baseball game when he hasn't any money," baseball's commissioner Kenesaw Mountain Landis bluntly observed, as game attendance in both the American League and National League plummeted from 10,132,262 in 1930 to 6,089,031 in 1933.

In 1933, the Goudey Gum Company packaged baseball cards with sticks of chewing gum. Billy Jurges was card number 225 of 239 cards. A 240th was added in 1934. *Author's collection.*

Baseball clubs naturally had to make up the loss of income, so teams suffered cuts in both team rosters and players' salaries. The average player salary of $7,500 in 1929 had slid to $6,009 in 1933. By 1939, it had climbed back up, though only to $7,306. But this was still "princely pay for the times," argues baseball historian David Quentin Voigt, as the typical industrial worker made just $1,421 in 1929, $1,064 in 1933 and $1,269 in 1939.

Although some baseball players held out for even more "princely" salaries, a Chicago newspaper noted with satisfaction in January 1935 that Billy Jurges had just signed his contract for the forthcoming season. The paper added that Jurges, now fully recovered from his bout of appendicitis, "foresees nothing that can strike him down during the tough campaign which the Cubs are bound to experience in 1935."[54]

And tough it was, for on July 5, 1935, the Cubs were mired in fourth place, ten and a half games behind the first-place New York Giants. On July 7, the scrappy Jurges led his team with "a perfect day at bat," as one sportswriter said, contributing two singles, two doubles and a walk as Chicago scored thirteen runs on fourteen hits in a 13–1 victory against the Pittsburgh Pirates. On September 4, the Cubs, now in third place, began an incredible September streak of wins as the bats "broke out like big metronomes." Ten days later, the team scored eight runs in the sixth inning during an 18–14 victory over the Brooklyn Dodgers, which lifted them into first place over the defending World Series champions, the St. Louis Cardinals. "Eleven in a row," the *Chicago Daily Tribune* gloated. "Now let's get that pennant."

The Cubs did not need to be told twice. On September 27, they clinched the National League pennant by winning the first game of a doubleheader against St. Louis and then taking the second game to extend their winning streak to twenty-one. The Cubs lost to the Cardinals the next day, 7–5, in eleven innings, but no matter; they had their pennant and they finished the season four games over St. Louis and eight and a half over the third-place New York Giants. They quickly packed their bags for Detroit, where they would face off against the American League's Tigers in the World Series.

Although the Cubs won the first game, 3–0, on October 2, the celebrating was short-lived. In the next game, the Tigers scored four runs in the first inning and stomped the Cubs, 8–3. The World Series moved to Chicago for the next three games, which were won respectively by the Tigers (6–5 in eleven innings), the Tigers (2–1) and the Cubs (3–1). The Tigers won the sixth game, played back in Detroit, by the score of 4–3, to capture the title.[55]

Buried in many of the game-day accounts were the Cubs' vitriolic taunts or "bench jockeying" directed toward the Tigers, and in particular to Hank Greenberg, an outstanding Jewish first baseman. Manager Charlie Grimm shrugged off what baseball historian Glenn Stout called the "abominable behavior" of the Cubs during the series. "Both clubs had great bench jockeys," Grimm recalled, "and I'll be the last one to deny that the great Hank Greenberg was our main target. Do you heckle a substitute or a star?"[56]

It was, however, more than mere heckling. The Cubs—notably Billy Herman, Charlie Root, Larry French and Billy Jurges—shouted obscenities and other coarse slurs at the Detroit players throughout the games, with Greenberg getting the worst of it. Greenberg said that during the first game "I learned that the Cubs were a bunch of tough SOBs…calling me Jew this and Jew that. Behind the plate was umpire George Moriarty; he walked over to the Cubs' bench and told them to stop riding me. They said it was none of his goddamned business and that they would ride me if they pleased."

Cub first baseman Phil Cavarretta remembered that "the language was kind of rough," with both sides yelling at each other. "We figured if we got on them a little heavy," Cavarretta explained, the Tigers would lose their concentration while batting. "I'd get up there and I'd hear it—'you dirty dago' and 'wop' and things like that.…This upsets you."

The Cubs themselves were none too happy in the third game, played on October 4, when George Moriarty called Cavarretta out in the sixth inning trying to steal second base. They protested the umpire's decision; he countered by ordering manager Charlie Grimm off the field. In the eighth inning, as the Cubs' "bench jockeys" rode Moriarty, he ejected Woody English and Tuck Stainback. Grimm complained to Commissioner Landis that after the Cubs objected to Moriarty's decisions, he retaliated by swearing at them. Choosing to ignore his own team's verbal assault on Hank Greenberg and other Tiger players, Grimm told a sportswriter that "I never have heard an umpire abuse members of a ball team with the language Moriarty used."[57]

In his twenty years with the Chicago Cubs (1934–53), Phil Cavarretta played in three World Series: 1935, 1938 and 1945. *Author's collection.*

Commissioner Landis ordered all of the parties involved to come to his office the next morning to tell him their sides of the story. As reported in one newspaper account, although the meeting was held behind the closed doors of the commissioner's office,

Moriarty and the players "could be heard accusing each other of opening fire." Landis announced after the meeting that he would take no action on the matter until after the World Series.

At the end of October, Woody English, Billy Herman, Billy Jurges and George Moriarty were each fined $200 for using "vile and unprintable" language, while Charlie Grimm was fined $200 for refusing Moriarty's order to leave the game and go to the team's clubhouse. Detroit player Hank Greenberg contended that Moriarty was unjustly punished. "The charges against the Cubs were well founded," he said, "but there was no justice in fining Moriarty. I wish I had been called in to testify in the case."

When Billy Herman was asked how many words he used in his argument with Moriarty, the Chicago ballplayer quickly retorted, "I used all of 'em."[58]

Billy Jurges was looking forward to working on his hitting during the 1936 spring training regimen. Not only had he wrapped up the previous season with a lackluster .241 batting average, but he had also struck out in the bottom of the ninth inning in the last game of the World Series, stranding his teammate Stan Hack on third base with no outs. "No one has to tell me that a fielder can't make the big money in baseball unless he can pound the ball with a bat," he told reporters. "I know how important hitting is and I get over-anxious and it's the pressing that spoils everything."

Jurges was always competitive, and he might have been over-anxious on April 30 when he hit a triple in the seventh inning of a game against the Brooklyn Dodgers. While sliding into third base, he rammed his right elbow into the ground, pulling the tendons of his arm and injuring a bone. The Cubs thought he would be out for the rest of the season, but he was back in the lineup on May 30 in a doubleheader against the Pittsburgh Pirates. Showing almost no trace of any arm damage, he managed to hit two singles and a double.

Although the Cubs were tied for first place with the St. Louis Cardinals at the end of June, a hitting slump took its toll on their league standing. They went into a Labor Day doubleheader in third place, though only four games behind the first-place New York Giants. But two Chicago losses, coupled with two New York wins, dropped the Cubs to six games back, with just nineteen games left on their schedule. As the *Tribune* lamented, "Their faint hopes of repeating as National league champions became dimmer than ever." They finished the season tied with St. Louis for second place, five games back of the Giants.

There was one bright spot, however: Billy Jurges's efforts to bolster his hitting paid off, as he raised his batting average from .241 to .280.[59]

Jurges raised it even more in 1937; in fact, the Cubs led the National League offensively that year with their .287 batting average and proved to be a formidable force through much of the season. On August 1, they were six games in front of the second-place Giants, but by September, New York—thanks in part to the stellar pitching of future Hall of Famer Carl Hubbell—leaped past them to claim the top spot. The Cubs ended the year in second place, three games behind New York.

Jurges's batting average probably should have been higher, but he never fully recovered from a shoulder injury he had suffered when he slid into home plate during a game on August 7. "My arm was caught in back of me," he remembered decades later. "I tore up my shoulder, and it was never right after that....At the time, I was leading the league with a .340 average. That's the year I wound up with a .298."

It was also the year that the Cubs extensively renovated Wrigley Field. The bleachers were remodeled and expanded, and a new scoreboard was constructed in center field. Naturally, the Cubs had in mind that the renovations would lead to increased attendance at the ballpark, though as one Chicago sportswriter observed, "If the truth were known, the desire for scenic distinction probably was more of an incentive than the desire

A postcard of Wrigley Field in late 1937, shortly before the completion of the new scoreboard. *Author's collection.*

to spring the capacity of the field." That "scenic distinction" was even more apparent when the now iconic ivy on the outfield walls was planted in September 1937.[60]

In February 1938, Billy Jurges was still smarting over the Cubs' loss of the pennant to the Giants the year before. He said during an interview that the Cubs would have easily finished the season in first place if their best pitchers had not been either sick or injured. "We looked more like a hospital ward than a ball club," he groused. He added that "we were out in front and it looked like a romp until the ambulance started making daily stops." This year would be different, he vowed. "If the Cubs avoid injuries, we'll breeze in."

The Cubs' chances looked even better a couple of months later. Shortly before Opening Day, the Cubs made headlines across the country when Wrigley sent three players and $185,000 to the St. Louis Cardinals for their star pitcher, Jay Hanna "Dizzy" Dean. It was well known that Dean had injured his pitching arm in 1937, but many team owners and players felt that with his drive and determination he could still win games for a pennant-contending ball club. Manager Charlie Grimm, though conceding that the trade "doesn't mean that a pennant is a certainty," said of the deal, "It's a dandy." *Time* magazine, on the other hand, titled its article "Dizzy Trade" and referred to Dean as a "pampered super-pitcher" who had won just thirteen games in 1937 and lost ten.[61]

Dean made his debut on April 20, 1938, in Cincinnati. He allowed two runs and eight hits in six innings in a 10–4 drubbing of the Cincinnati Reds, and he pitched a 5–0 complete game against the Cardinals on April 24, yielding only four hits. The *New York Times* reported less than two weeks later, however, that Dean was "ordered to rest his salaried arm" after he was unable to finish a game on May 4 due to inflammation of the deltoid muscle. The Cubs' physician thought he could pitch in about a month, though it was not until July 17 that Dean would once again take the field for the Cubs. But when he did, he silenced his critics who thought his arm was gone by hurling a brilliant four-hit game to beat the Boston Bees, 3–1.[62]

The Cubs, however, were only in third place in the National League, and pennant hopes were fading. Phil Cavarretta thought that manager Charlie Grimm was getting "burnout" after years of devoting his life to the national pastime. "What Charlie's problem was, I don't know," Cavarretta said. "But he seemed to be losing his drive as far as the game was concerned." Others thought the popular, easygoing Grimm had little control over his players and blamed him for failing to reach the World Series in 1936 and

Pitcher Dizzy Dean joined the Chicago Cubs in April 1938 and helped them win a National League pennant later that fall. *Author's collection.*

1937. Cubs owner Philip K. Wrigley no doubt agreed and soon decided to switch managers. "Charlie Grimm has done a swell job," Wrigley said, "but I decided that a change would be best for the organization. Grimm gave us everything he had, but the club has not done as well as we felt it should."

Wrigley fired Grimm on July 20 and announced that catcher Charles Leo "Gabby" Hartnett would take his place as manager. Hartnett was a

Chicago Cub manager Charlie Grimm watches catcher Gabby Hartnett make a difficult billiards shot. *Author's collection.*

logical choice. He had joined the Cubs in 1922 and was widely regarded as a leader on the club, one of baseball's premier catchers and a potent batter. (His batting average of .354 was the team's best in 1937.) "To a generation of North Side fans, Hartnett was nothing less than an idol," declared sportswriter Shirley Povich.[63]

Hartnett's Cubs split a doubleheader in his managerial debut on July 21, defeating the Brooklyn Dodgers in the first game, 5–2, and losing the second, 1–0. Two days later, during a game against the New York Giants, Billy Jurges was caught between second and third bases and tagged out by Giant shortstop Dick Bartell. Jurges crashed into him, and both players started swinging at each other. Bartell relates in his autobiography, aptly titled *Rowdy Richard*, that "for some reason Jurges and I didn't get along. I don't mean like oil and water. I mean like gasoline and matches.…He was a pretty emotional guy, and I was hot-tempered. Every time one of us slid into the other at second base, we came up fighting. We were alike in one way: we both hated anybody wearing the other uniform."

The *Chicago Daily Tribune* remarked that as far as baseball fights went, "The Jurges-Bartell imbroglio was above the average.…Eventually every member of both teams arrived and the fun stopped." The two belligerent players were tossed from the game, and Chicago went on to defeat New York by the score of 3–1.

The Cubs could have used some of Jurges's intensity as they began their drive for the pennant. Although they won five of their first six games with Hartnett as manager, their record after twenty-four more was just 15-15. On September 3, they lost a doubleheader to the Cincinnati Reds and were in fourth place in the National League, seven games behind the Pittsburgh Pirates.

But pennant hopes soon returned. The Cubs won their next six games—including a doubleheader with Pittsburgh—which vaulted Chicago to second place and shrunk the Pirates' lead to three and a half games. In late September, the Cubs swept a four-game series against the Philadelphia Phillies and a three-game set against the St. Louis Cardinals, setting the stage for what the *Chicago Daily Tribune* called the "September World Series": a dramatic three-game showdown against Pittsburgh at Wrigley Field. The Pirates held only a slim one-and-a-half-game lead over Chicago, and each team had but seven games left to play.

The "thrills never abated," the *Tribune* told its readers, as a sore-armed Dizzy Dean, in his first start since August 20, pitched eight and two-thirds heroic innings in a 2–1 victory in the first game of the series on September 27. He obviously was in pain throughout the afternoon, but Dean said afterward that "I wasn't going to have that stop me from winning the greatest game of my life." In their previous twenty-two games, the Cubs had won eighteen, lost three and tied one, and they were now just a mere one-half game out of first place.[64]

The following day would mark Gabby Hartnett's own greatest game. The 34,465 raucous fans who crowded into Wrigley Field knew that a Cub victory would put them atop the National League standings. The Pirates had taken a 5–3 lead in the eighth inning, but Cub Ripper Collins scored in the Chicago half of the inning, and Billy Jurges walked and then tied the game, making it 5–5.

Pitcher Charlie Root easily retired the Pittsburgh batters in the ninth. But dusk had settled in, and the umpires agreed that if the game was tied after the ninth inning, it would be called on account of darkness and would be replayed the next day as part of a doubleheader. The Cubs wanted to avoid that scenario; their pitchers were already worn out, and it would surely be difficult for the team to win both of these crucial games.

Chicago Cubs News

VOLUME 6, NO. 4 WRIGLEY FIELD, JULY 22, 1941 CHICAGO, ILLINOIS

"CHARLIE ROOT DAY"

August 10, 1941

The Cubs and their fans honor the team's longtime pitcher on "Charlie Root Day," held at Wrigley Field on August 10, 1941. *From* Chicago Cubs News, *July 22, 1941.*

Chicago's batters were down to their last three outs, and it was getting "darker every second," according to the *Tribune* sportswriter. Pirate pitcher Mace Brown "was firing them in as hard as he could to cash in on the darkness." Brown easily got the first two batters out, and then Gabby Hartnett strode to the plate. It appeared that he did not even see the ball as two strikes whizzed by him. With daylight almost gone, on a no-ball, two-strike count, Brown threw a curve ball. Hartnett drove it into the left-field bleachers for a stunning 6–5 Cubs victory. "The crowd was in an uproar, absolutely gone wild," recalled Pirate outfielder Paul Waner some twenty-five years later. "They ran onto the field like a bunch of maniacs, and his teammates and the crowd and all were mobbing Hartnett, and piling on top of him, and throwing him up in the air, and everything you could think of. I've never seen anything like it before or since."

Neither had anyone else. "We surrender to inadequacy," is how sportswriter John P. Carmichael began his next day's column for the *Chicago Daily News*. "This Cub-Pirate pennant fight has gone far beyond our poor power to picture in words." There is little doubt that no home run in Cub history has matched Hartnett's "Homer in the Gloamin'" (a phrase purportedly coined by Associated Press sportswriter Earl Hilligan as a takeoff on the 1911 popular song "Roamin' in the Gloamin'"), and Gabby himself called the hit and the Cubs' victory "the two greatest things that ever happened to me in my life."[65]

As for the dispirited Pirates, "That home run took all the fight out of us," Paul Waner admitted. "It broke our hearts." Chicago crushed Pittsburgh in the last game of the series, 10–1, and went on to win the National League pennant. The Cubs squared off in the World Series against their old foes from 1932, the New York Yankees. The Yankees, though, clearly had both more fight and stronger hearts than had the Pirates. To the satisfaction of Joe McCarthy—whom the Cubs had summarily fired in 1930—the New Yorkers once again thoroughly dominated the Chicago North Siders, taking the first two games in Chicago by the scores of 3–1 and 6–3, and the third and fourth games in New York, 5–2 and 8–3.[66]

Cub manager Gabby Hartnett was both disappointed and embarrassed after his team did not win even one game in the World Series, and he vowed there would be changes in the Cubs' lineup the next year. "There'll be a clean sweep of the ball club," he told reporters after the train bearing the players rolled into Chicago's LaSalle Street station. "That includes outfielders, infielders and pitchers. I'm not mentioning any names but there'll be a different ball club on the North Side."

After Philip K. Wrigley selected Gabby Hartnett (*right*) as Cub manager in July 1938, Hartnett appointed second baseman Billy Herman (*left*) captain of the team. *Author's collection.*

Billy Jurges had good reason to believe his own position on the team was secure. Few people knew that when Philip Wrigley wanted to hire a new manager in July 1938, the Cubs' owner had first offered *him* the job, but Jurges had turned it down in favor of Hartnett. "Mr. Wrigley," Billy had told him, "Gabby Hartnett has played for you for nearly 20 years. I think he should be your manager, if you have decided to replace Charlie Grimm."

Wrigley took Jurges's advice, and during the stretch drive toward the pennant, Hartnett kept telling Billy how glad he was that his friend was on the team and how much he was looking forward to working with him the next year. In the off-season, though, Hartnett changed his mind. Perhaps he viewed Jurges as a threat to his own managerial career, for as the shortstop remembered years later, "The first trade Gabby made that winter sent me to the Giants."

Billy's teammates were incredulous when they learned that he was traded. "We all talked about it in spring training," recalled Phil Cavarretta. "Billy

Jurges would go out, play hard, go through a brick wall for you....Why trade a Billy Jurges? We couldn't understand it, really."

Jurges couldn't, either, but at least now he would be closer to his family in Brooklyn. "I think the change in scenery will do me a world of good," he told a reporter. With his typical single-minded resolve, he added, "I'm ready to play my head off to bring that flag to the [Giants'] Polo Grounds."[67]

Billy certainly got off to a promising start with his new team. One sportswriter observed in March 1939 that Jurges had long been one of the National League's best shortstops, and "this Spring he...looks primed for his best season. Right now he is moving at top form." The 1939 baseball season was not even two weeks old when the New York Giants' infielder paved the way for a May 4 win against the St. Louis Cardinals. "Billy Jurges," exulted the *New York Times*, "closing an afternoon of brilliant defensive play, started the Giant victory drive in the eighth with a rousing three-base clout to deep right center."

Although the Giants finished fifth in the National League in 1939 (the Cubs placed fourth), Jurges raised his batting average from .245 in 1938 to .285. He was chosen for the National League's All-Star team in 1940—he had also been selected in 1937 and 1939—but after he was hit on the back of the head by a high curve ball on June 23 and suffered a concussion, he missed much of the rest of the 1940 season. As a direct result of Jurges's "beaning," baseball officials and physicians began seriously discussing how head protectors could prevent such injuries.[68]

Billy Jurges played in the 1932, 1935 and 1938 World Series. He was chosen for the National League's All-Star team in 1937, 1939 and 1940. *Author's collection.*

Jurges stayed with the Giants through the 1945 season. After they released him late that year, he joined the Boston Braves as a coach and utility infielder (that is, someone who could play several positions in the infield as needed). The Braves let him go in March 1946, and he immediately returned to the Cubs as a utility infielder, where he wound up his last two seasons in the major leagues. "I was happy to come back," Billy reminisced years later. "I liked Chicago. Chicago is a great town and they're great fans. They're wonderful fans."[69]

Jurges both coached and played for the Cubs in 1947. His last game was at Wrigley Field on September 9, notable for Cliff Aberson's grand slam home run in the bottom of the eighth inning that turned a potential 3–0 loss to the Brooklyn Dodgers into a 4–3 Cub victory. Manager Charlie Grimm put Billy in as shortstop in the top of the ninth inning, and he caught a pop-up to record the last out of the game—a fitting way to cap his long, successful career.

Jurges stayed on in Chicago as a coach for a time, but late in 1948, he left baseball to enter the business world, joining the firm of A.G. Spalding & Bros. as a member of the baseball promotion staff and a liaison officer with eastern teams. He emphasized in an interview that he took the position at the company not because he was tired of baseball but "because, at the age of 40, I had not landed one of the very good jobs in the majors, and I had decided not to be a member of the army of the knocked-around." As Billy picked up a baseball and looked at it, he mused, "Beautiful creation—and now I won't be doing anything with or without it except helping to sell it."[70]

Jurges apparently did not find selling baseballs as rewarding as demonstrating how to hit and field them. In April 1950, he signed on as manager of the Cleveland Indians' farm club in Cedar Rapids, Iowa, hoping that the job would lead to a more prominent position in the Indians' organization. Unfortunately for his career plans, his team placed fifth in the league at the end of the season, and in October, Billy was let go as manager.

Jurges then went into business with his brother-in-law in Washington, D.C., serving as a manufacturer's representative handling government contracts. In February 1952, he used his vacation time to join the Boston Braves in Bradenton, Florida, as an infield coach during spring training.

A year later, the Hagerstown (Maryland) Braves, the farm club of the Milwaukee Braves, hired Jurges as team manager. On July 12, 1953, he made an "auspicious debut as manager," as noted in the pages of *The Sporting News*, beating the Lynchburg, Virginia team in eleven innings, 8–7.

After his Braves ended the season in second place in their league, Billy was still hoping to land a job working in the major leagues. He was considered for a coaching position with the Washington Senators for 1955, but the job went to former Senator player Ellis Clary. "It's strange," wrote *The Sporting News*, that "some club doesn't latch onto a heady guy like Jurgie."[71]

"Jurgie" always regretted turning down Philip Wrigley's job offer in 1938 to manage the Cubs. "I've spent every year since kicking myself," he would comment ruefully. "In the majors, only a very few land the big jobs. You wait and wait for the lightning to strike, and so often it hits in other places." It took the Boston Red Sox slipping to last place in the American League on June 29, 1959, for that big bolt of lightning finally to strike.

After the Red Sox had ended the 1954 season in fourth place, owner Tom Yawkey fired manager Lou Boudreau and hired Mike "Pinky" Higgins, who had been in charge of Boston's farm system for eight years. Higgins, unfortunately, did little better than Boudreau, and the Red Sox finished fourth in 1955 and 1956 and third in 1957 and 1958.

Yawkey fired Higgins on July 3, 1959, and Boston general manager Bucky Harris signed Jurges for the rest of that season and the following one. Billy immediately packed his bags so he could catch a plane for Baltimore, where his new team was playing the Orioles in a four-game series. The Orioles, unfortunately, spoiled his debut as manager on July 4 by getting thirteen hits and four home runs in an 11–5 victory—the seventh straight loss for the Red Sox. The famed but aging Ted Williams had gone into the game hitting only .201, and Jurges had dropped him from third place to sixth in the batting order, the lowest he had batted since 1939, his rookie year. Williams responded to the move by securing two hits and batting in two runs.[72]

The new Red Sox manager took the defeat gracefully and applauded his players' performance on the field. He was encouraged after the Red Sox swept the Orioles in a doubleheader the next day by scores of 9–0 and 6–3. Jurges told interviewers that "the Red Sox have no business being in last place. It's my job to get them to relax and to get them moving. And there's only one place to go. That's up and I'm sure we'll go up."

Unfortunately, hustling and moving up were not words in the Red Sox vocabulary. A decided air of complacency seemed to surround the team, and many players did not care whether they won or lost as long as they had fun. An anonymous ballplayer (rumored to be right fielder Jackie Jensen) revealed in a July 24 article in Boston's *Christian Science Monitor* that many key players had "the wrong attitude" and they were "simply going through the motions, playing out the season." He added that "I'd like to see a manager here who is tough, real tough. The club needs shaking up. I thought perhaps Billy Jurges could do it. But now I'm not so sure."

The gritty and hard-playing Jurges would never simply go through the motions, and as a manager he would not tolerate that attitude from any player. That evening, he held a team meeting at which he also invited coaches, newspaper writers and radio announcers. In front of everyone he declared: "I challenge the player who gave that interview to stand up and tell us all about it." Naturally, no one said a word. The tense situation in the

As manager of the Boston Red Sox from 1959 to 1960, Billy Jurges compiled a record of fifty-nine wins and sixty-three losses. *Author's collection.*

clubhouse, along with the problem of numerous sick and injured players, had overshadowed the team's historic addition of Elijah Jerry "Pumpsie" Green to the Red Sox roster. The African American ballplayer had debuted as a pinch-runner on July 21, thereby completing the racial integration of all major-league teams.

The rest of the season remained a rocky one for the new manager. The Red Sox ended the year in fifth place in the eight-team American League, with seventy-five wins and seventy-nine losses. But a team's finish at the end of the year does not reveal the whole picture. With Jurges's forty-four wins and thirty-six losses in 1959, sportswriter Shirley Povich thought he did a "superior" job as manager. (Pinky Higgins's record in the first half of the season was only 31-42.)[73]

By the start of the 1960 season, however, Billy saw few reasons for optimism. Ted Williams was still plagued by the same stiff neck that had limited the left fielder's batting average to just .254 in 1959 (he had hit a league-leading .328 the year before). Right fielder Jackie Jensen had led the league in 1959 with 112 runs batted in, but in January, he had announced his retirement so he could spend more time with his family. "I'm quite concerned about the outfield," Billy said in the spring, adding that he also had doubts about who could handle first base.

The team's deficiencies were soon readily apparent. Jurges reportedly "hit the ceiling" during spring training in Scottsdale, Arizona, when the Red Sox lost their fourth straight pre-season game. During his years with the Cubs, Billy was known for his ability to swiftly turn double plays, and he was particularly upset when in two successive games his players botched their chances to record two quick outs. "A big leaguer makes the double play," he fumed, after second baseman Pumpsie Green fumbled the ball.

The manager's relations with the press did not give him much satisfaction, either. Journalists—including an obvious pro–Mike Higgins faction—questioned his strategy on the field and reported that players openly criticized his managerial style. One sportswriter noted that Jurges worked hard and had a "tremendous desire" to win ball games, but to be a successful manager "he must have full control of his ball club." The writer acknowledged that Jurges was trying to gain that control, but he also needed the respect of the ballplayers, and "without it there is much difficulty." To earn that respect, the reporter added, he needed to talk to the ballplayers and straighten out any misunderstandings.[74]

Billy admitted that he was "shocked" by the newspaper reports and on April 26 decided to clear the air. "I called the players together," Jurges said, "and asked them to state their gripes. Nobody did. I feel that is the only way to get this thing straightened out….I had no idea that anything like this was going on and I just can't believe it….They've hustled, they've given me 100 percent cooperation and I haven't heard a single complaint."

One unidentified player said that Jurges was not respected because of his hasty decisions on the field, continual juggling of lineups and "unsound tactics." (He did not elaborate on just what those tactics were.) On the other hand, some team members, including Ted Williams, dismissed the reports of dissension and expressed confidence in Jurges: "It's those damn Boston writers again," snapped Williams. "They're always starting trouble. What do they want the fellow to do? He's doing the best he can. And he's doing a damn good job….He's all right in my book."

Billy was also all right in the books of some other Boston sportswriters, who recognized that the cards were stacked against him from the beginning simply because he replaced Mike Higgins, the "pal" of many reporters. One sympathetic journalist also reasoned that "the Red Sox started falling apart five years ago," and they now contained "playing personnel [who are] just about the least competent in the entire [Tom] Yawkey regime."[75]

Left fielder Ted Williams, one of the greatest hitters in the history of baseball, played for Red Sox manager Billy Jurges. *Wikimedia Commons.*

A 7–5 victory against the New York Yankees on April 26 silenced some of Billy's critics, and a calm clubhouse meeting brought players around to his side. "We went over the hitters," said one team member, "and Jurges said, 'If any of you don't like what I'm doing I wish you'd come out and tell me. We can straighten it out.'"

The players were impressed that their manager had made his point deliberately and quietly, with no anger or finger-pointing. In addition, his strategic defensive moves during the game paid off, and Pumpsie Green's well-executed double play helped seal the win. Even Billy's detractors in the press praised the manager. "Jurges' handling of a ticklish situation was excellent," wrote one. "No panic, no histrionics, merely a calm, sensible approach to a problem that has confronted many managers before in baseball."

The Red Sox won four games in a row between May 6 and May 12, but soon, the losses started piling up again. On May 22, the Sox lost a doubleheader to the Tigers in Detroit, sending Boston to last place in the American League. Two days later, the Kansas City Athletics handed the Red Sox their tenth loss in a row. On May 25, the Red Sox finally snapped their losing streak, and Jurges commended his players after the game for their "hustling and giving the team their best on the field." One of the men told a reporter, "You couldn't blame Billy for the way things have been going… He may have made one or two wrong guesses, but most of the time he's tried everything anyone could to shake us out of the slump."[76]

But the strain on Jurges was obviously taking its toll. On May 14, the Red Sox had been only one game out of first place. By June 7, the team was in the cellar and had won just five of the last twenty-five games. Soon after Billy had accepted the managerial job in early June 1959, he had told friends, "I don't think I'll let the tension get me." That note of cheerful optimism was now replaced by, "No job is worth this pressure." On June 8, the Red Sox announced that the team physician and a Boston internal medicine specialist had examined Jurges and prescribed complete rest. (The specialist found him to be "completely exhausted from a fruitless task.") Red Sox coach Del Baker was immediately appointed the team's interim manager.[77]

The ball club did not indicate in its announcement of the new manager if Jurges was on his way out, but most savvy baseball people assumed that was the case; sure enough, owner Tom Yawkey fired him on June 10. Billy was gracious when he received the news, publicly stating that "it's best for all…for Mr. Yawkey's sake and for the fans in Boston. There's a lot to be done in Boston and the new fellow must have a free hand. Maybe he can do better than I did."

Jurges's Red Sox won fifteen games and lost twenty-seven in 1960. This gave him, for the years 1959 and 1960, a disappointing major-league managerial record of 59-63 and a winning percentage of just .484. To make matters even worse, Yawkey then rehired Mike Higgins, whom Jurges had replaced a year earlier. Jurges told an interviewer while reflecting on his brief time in Boston that "when you become a manager, you have to have a team that is coming up. All my players on the Red Sox were finishing up their careers and there was not much I could do there."[78]

Billy, though, had plenty he could do in other baseball jobs, and he had no plans to just retire and quietly go home. In early July, he joined the Baltimore Orioles, scouting and evaluating the National League teams in preparation for interleague trading in the fall. For years, the Jurges family had lived in northern Virginia, and in the spring of 1961, he became a scout for the newly formed New York Mets, primarily working in the Maryland-Virginia area. Early the following year, he signed on as a coach with the other new National League team, the Houston Colt .45s (later the Astros).

In November 1968 the Washington Senators announced that they had hired Jurges as a scout, assigned to appraise possible high draft players. Billy had been reluctant to leave the Houston club, but he wanted to work closer to his home. "Houston was very good to me," he said, "but they understood my desire to get a job nearer home. Of course, I'll still be away a lot but I'll also manage to get home more often."[79]

During his post-playing years as a scout, teams respected Jurges's shrewd assessments of prospective ballplayers and his ability at determining if a man could make it in professional baseball. In the late 1970s, he worked for the Seattle Mariners, and in November 1978, the Cubs persuaded him to return to his old club for a few more years.

In addition to his work as a scout, Jurges was known as an excellent instructor on the field. More than one Hall of Famer would later acknowledge his debt to the former shortstop. Decades before Eddie Mathews was enshrined in

Cooperstown, he was a struggling player for the Boston Braves. In 1952, the team brought Jurges in to coach young infielders during spring training, and he found an apt pupil in Mathews. While Billy was with the Washington Senators, he had similar success in the spring of 1959 with Harmon Killebrew. Jurges not only helped young players learn new baseball skills and techniques, but he also tried to instill in them his intense drive and passion for the game. "All I ever wanted to do was play baseball," he reminisced years later. "And once the game started, all I wanted to do was win."

But the games had to end sometime. Jurges finally stopped scouting, coaching and teaching when his wife's health began declining in the early 1980s. Professional baseball was such a significant aspect of his life for more than a half century, but now the time had come for him to retire.[80]

7
LAST YEARS

Cubs, Giants, good year or bad year, I have never failed to do my best, to play out to the limit.
—Billy Jurges, The Sporting News, *December 15, 1948*

Vi had friends, she was sociable. Her interests were baseball and movies. She liked to have a good time.
—interview with Michael Prescott, January 24, 2020

Baseball meant a great deal to Billy Jurges, but his family always remained uppermost in his mind. When he accepted the job as manager of the Red Sox, a reporter asked him if he would leave his home in Virginia and move to Boston. "No, indeed," he immediately replied. "It has nothing to do with Boston, which I think is a lovely city. It's just that my daughter and granddaughter live in Alexandria, Va." He especially wanted to stay in touch with his granddaughter, "Pinky," and said that "if I moved to Boston permanently, I wouldn't see Pinky."

In later years, he also got to spend time with his grandson, who as a young boy accompanied Jurges on a few baseball scouting trips. "We traveled to Baltimore, Boston, and Montreal to scout major league players," Bill Price remembered. "He taught me how to rate different aspects of a player's game. I also had the chance to meet a lot of the players in those cities. I will never forget [Boston Red Sox player] Carl Yastrzemski sticking his fingers

Former Cubs Charlie Grimm, Billy Herman, Billy Jurges and Stan Hack at the annual dinner of the Boston Baseball Writers Association, January 28, 1965. *Associated Press.*

through the backstop screen at Fenway Park to shake my hand. Although these stories may not be as much about Billy Jurges as they are about me, it goes to show how much he loved baseball and how much he loved to share the game with me and others."

One of those with whom Jurges talked baseball was Ronald Reagan, who broadcast Cub games for radio station WHO in Des Moines, Iowa, during the 1930s. Reagan would socialize with the ballplayers—who always called him by his nickname, "Dutch"—during spring training on Catalina Island. Recalled Jurges:

> *One night we were in spring training in California, and we were all supposed to get together, but Dutch didn't show up. Finally, he got there around 10, and told us he had been to Hollywood to take a screen test. He wore glasses then, and we all kidded him. "You, take a screen test? As ugly as you are?"*

> *Well, he told us he had signed a contract with a movie company for $275 a week. And that was the end of Dutch as a broadcaster. He was a terrific guy to be around, though. He didn't smoke, or drink, and he didn't cuss.*
>
> *I still hear from him once in a while. He called me when my wife of 51 years passed away in 1984.*[81]

Jurges had quit the baseball life in the early 1980s to take care of his ailing wife. Several years after Mary died, he remarried, and he spent his retirement with his second wife, Phyllis, and family members. "I enjoy the good life in Largo, Fla.," he said in an interview published in 1988. "There's a park adjacent to our house and we play poker, pinochle, horse shoes and dance." He and Phyllis traveled together, and he would visit with baseball players who lived near him, such as his former fellow infielder on the Cubs, Phil Cavarretta. He observed that baseball had helped make his life happy and fulfilling, but at the same time, he had worked hard to promote the sport so others could enjoy it as well. "Cubs, Giants, good year or bad year," he said, "I have never failed to do my best, to play out to the limit. Baseball has done well by me. I have done all I could for baseball."

Although he was not a powerful hitter, the slick-fielding Jurges more than compensated for that with his solid defensive skills. Indeed, during his seventeen years in the major leagues (1931–47), he led National League shortstops in fielding percentage four times (1932, 1935, 1937 and 1939) and once in double plays turned (1935). He batted .258 in 1,816 games, collecting 1,613 hits.

Jurges was diagnosed with cancer in 1991. He entered the hospital on January 27, 1997, and died a few weeks later on March 3 at age eighty-eight. He was cremated and some of his ashes were spread in various locations near his home in Florida that were significant and meaningful to him. "Pop's" ashes also quietly made their way to a special place in Chicago, according to his grandson. "Although I was denied permission by the Cubs to spread some of Pop's ashes inside Wrigley Field," Bill Price recalled, "I managed to do so stealthily prior to a Cubs game. I would have liked to have spread his ashes at shortstop. However, the best I could do was in front of the third baseline box seats near the Cubs' dugout."

Fourteen months after Billy's death, his widow, Phyllis, reminisced that "he was a wonderful man—a Real Major Leaguer! He is terribly missed by me, family, and friends.…He was a GREAT story-teller—and how I miss them." She added that his fans and the people who knew him could be "thankful for his 70+ years in Baseball. I'm thankful for our wonderful 10 years."

During a conversation about her father's baseball career, Jurges's only child, Suzanne Price, said that he loved baseball and particularly loved playing with the Cubs. "He was good friends with everybody there. And he was friends with everybody after he left the Cubs, too. And even after he retired, he was good friends with many of them."

She said that Billy gave her son much of his baseball memorabilia, including his 1938 Cub jersey and pants. ("That wool uniform—how they could play wearing that, I don't know.") She added that over the years Billy had collected many autographed baseballs, "which would be worth a fortune had he kept them, but he donated them to the War effort [World War II]. He was quite a man, my father, so he didn't keep anything like that. He gave it away to the War effort."

When Price was asked if she knew that Violet Popovich had shot her father in 1932, she said she was familiar with the incident but that when she was growing up, "It was never mentioned in our house. Never."[82]

By 1940, Violet and her mother, Margaret Heindl, had moved from Chicago and settled in Los Angeles, California. Violet loved the warm southern California climate—a far cry from the harsh weather of Chicago—and looked forward to her new life with enthusiasm and confidence. She always considered herself a professional singer and soon had photographs taken of herself to try to get back on the stage. Unfortunately, despite the glamor shots, she saw few opportunities for launching a West Coast singing career. In 1947, she married Charley Retzlaff, a former heavyweight prizefighter from North Dakota who had fought out of Duluth, Minnesota. (How and where she met him is unknown.) Retzlaff's first professional fight had been in 1929, and his prowess in the ring earned him the nickname the "Duluth Dynamiter"—at least it did until January 17, 1936, when a young Joe Louis knocked him out in less than two minutes. Retzlaff retired in 1940 and returned to his family farm in the small North Dakota community of Leonard. After his marriage, he expected his wife to enjoy rural life as much as he did, but according to her nephew, Mark Prescott, Violet was "bored to death" on the farm, and she stayed only a few weeks before moving back to Los Angeles.

She and her husband, however, did not get divorced, and they remained on friendly terms. In 1962, they spent Thanksgiving at the Prescott home in Beverly Hills, where Violet announced at the dinner table that she and Charley had spent part of that day sunbathing nude. "That comment

Left: By 1940, Violet Popovich and her mother, Margaret, had left Chicago and settled in Los Angeles. *MA&LJ Prescott Joint Trust.*

Right: After Violet Popovich moved to California, she had promotional photographs taken of herself, as she hoped to pursue a singing career. *MA&LJ Prescott Joint Trust.*

caused quite a stir," Mark Prescott recalled. "Charley was very embarrassed, my father blew up, and words went flying."

The gregarious Popovich was certainly not at a loss for other friends. She once caught the eye of motion-picture star John Wayne, who struck up a conversation with Violet at a cocktail lounge near where she worked and drove her home. If he harbored any lascivious hopes of getting comfortable and staying a while, they were soon dashed by the presence of her mother, who was waiting up for her. Violet still found herself attracted to baseball players, and she resumed her friendship with Al Lopez (who, interestingly enough, had warned Billy Jurges about her "bad reputation" in 1932). Prescott particularly remembered going to a White Sox game with his aunt when he was nine years old. Lopez, then manager of the team, came into the stands to chat with them, bringing a baseball that he autographed for the boy.[83]

Mark's cousin lived with their aunt for a year, from April 1969 to April 1970, and enjoyed her company and pleasant, engaging disposition.

Left: In 1947, Violet Popovich married Charley Retzlaff, a former heavyweight prizefighter known as the "Duluth Dynamiter." The marriage failed, but they remained friends. *MA&LJ Prescott Joint Trust.*

Right: Violet Popovich (about age forty), enjoys a playful moment with her nephew Mark. *MA&LJ Prescott Joint Trust.*

Michael Prescott remembered that "although my aunt's childhood was not easy—she was in an orphanage in the 1920s—she did not talk about it. She was easygoing and upbeat. She was never depressed or melancholy. Vi had friends, she was sociable. Her interests were baseball and movies. She liked to have a good time. She struck me as a very normal person, and I had no idea she had shot the 1932 Cubs shortstop."

Popovich lived in the Studio City neighborhood of Los Angeles and worked in the color film production department of Paramount Studios. She was not well off financially, and following her retirement she asked a man and his wife to live with her to help with expenses. When she could not afford to pay the property taxes on her house, she agreed to sell it to the couple on the condition that she could stay there. As evidenced by the Jurges shooting and her marriage—in fact, probably both her marriages—Violet had a tendency to not particularly think through major decisions. In this case, she failed to consult a lawyer to protect her legal rights, and after

Left: Violet Popovich, wearing shorts and a cape, strikes a pose for a Los Angeles photographer. *MA&LJ Prescott Joint Trust.*

Below: Violet Popovich sits on a jeep at Paramount Studios in Los Angeles, where she was employed in the color film production department. *MA&LJ Prescott Joint Trust.*

the two took possession of the house they changed the locks, effectively evicting her.

Violet Popovich spent her final years in a nursing home. What she lacked in money, she made up for in buoyant spirits, and she enjoyed regaling both residents and staff with stories about her past as a singer and showgirl. She died at age eighty-eight—as had Billy Jurges—on February 25, 2000, and was buried in Los Angeles's Forest Lawn Memorial Park in Hollywood Hills. (Her father had died in Chicago in 1945 and her mother twelve years later in Los Angeles.)[84]

Like Violet, the Hotel Carlos had its share of tough times. The building was relatively new when she and the ballplayers were frequent guests, and 1930s postcards touted it as the "Homelike Hotel." As the decades passed, however, the residential hotel lost all vestiges of "home" as it gradually fell into disrepair. Its name was changed to the Sheffield House Hotel, though the six-story building retained the imposing stone entryway with "Hotel Carlos" elaborately carved above the door.

Persons with low incomes or poor credit histories could inexpensively rent rooms by the day, week or month as the Sheffield required no leases or security deposits. Cub fans in town for a weekend, looking for a cheap hotel near the ballpark, often checked in but were usually dismayed by the mildew, peeling paint, dirty bathrooms and stained upholstery in the 130 units. "The place was a dive," according to Chicago Cubs historian Ed Hartig. "It was rundown and unkempt, and passersby would often cross to the other side of the street when walking by it."

As urban renewal and gentrification altered America's cityscape, the Sheffield and other single-room occupancy hotels were either torn down or repurposed. Real estate company BJB Properties purchased the Sheffield House Hotel in 2011, and that summer, the 105 residents received notices to vacate the premises. In 2014, the completely remodeled and renamed "3834 N Sheffield"—a "once hip apartment hotel for Cubs players"—offered studio apartments to upscale professionals. The owners announced that the new hardwood floors, granite countertops and stainless-steel appliances "modernize the gorgeous vintage details that remain from a glorious and distant era."

One of those remaining vintage details was the stone entryway, its ornate "Hotel Carlos" carving still welcoming all who passed through the door.[85]

The renovated "3834 N Sheffield," with original carved entryway and "Hotel Carlos" name. Billy Jurges's room is still there—on the top floor, far right. *Christina A. Reynen.*

Cub fans regularly walk past that door on their way to Wrigley Field. Some with a sense of their team's history have probably glanced inside and wondered: Had Violet Popovich really intended to kill Billy Jurges when she slipped a revolver in her purse and quietly went upstairs to his room? She denied it at the time, but the letter she had left in her own hotel room clearly indicates that murder had been on her mind; furthermore, why else would she and Betty have gone target shooting in back of the hotel on July 5? From the very beginning, the police had doubted Violet's story that she had meant to use the gun only on herself. As it turned out, they were correct. Her nephew Mark Prescott said that years later she confided to his mother that she had, indeed, gone to room 509 intending to shoot the ballplayer. As Violet told her sister-in-law, "I was very angry and I wanted to kill him."

Violet's turbulent upbringing and abusive father do not excuse her behavior, but they help explain why she wanted a close relationship with Billy. Baseball has long had its share of fans who fantasize about players. Some women are looking for romance, while others "collect one-night stands like baseball cards." Unlike many of the sport's groupies or "Baseball Annies" (a term memorialized by Annie Savoy in the 1988 motion picture *Bull Durham*), Violet sought intimacy and commitment rather than sex. Ed Hartig believes that "she was desperate for attention and affection—certainly not getting that from her family life, especially from her father and a failed marriage. I think she felt that she finally would find it with Billy Jurges—though if it hadn't been Jurges, she likely would have latched onto almost any ballplayer."

The Cubs' 1932 baseball season was a succession of adverse circumstances, but an observer could say it was also a year of multiple "what ifs." What if Billy Jurges had not been shot? What if Mark Koenig had been awarded a full share of the World Series bonus money? What if the Cubs and the Yankees had not exchanged so many heated insults prior to Babe Ruth stepping up to the plate in Game Three? When Violet pulled the trigger in the Hotel Carlos, her bullets not only struck Jurges but also had a domino effect on the Cubs, Mark Koenig, the 1932 pennant race, the division of the World Series money and Babe Ruth's "Called Shot." With Billy's recovery uncertain, the Cubs had brought in another shortstop, and as Hartig contends, "The shooting of Jurges opened the door for Koenig to become a Cub and baseball legend."

The shooting made Violet something of a legend as well. In 1949, nineteen-year-old Chicagoan Ruth Ann Steinhagen, who had a "twisted fascination" with former Cub (and then Philadelphia Phillie) Eddie Waitkus, shot him in his room at Chicago's Edgewater Beach Hotel. Ironically, Waitkus and

Jurges had played together for two years, and Waitkus had hit a double in Jurges's last game on September 9, 1947. Author Bernard Malamud rarely discussed the sources for his works, but it seems likely that one or both of the two attempted murders inspired him to include a passage in his 1952 novel, *The Natural*, in which a woman shoots ballplayer Roy Hobbs.

The Natural and that scene continue to live on today, thanks to the hit 1984 motion picture starring Robert Redford as Hobbs. And Violet Popovich will remain a part of baseball, too, inextricably linked to the 1932 season and one of the most unusual and memorable episodes in the sport's history.[86]

ABBREVIATIONS

BDE = *Brooklyn* (NY) *Daily Eagle*
CA = *Chicago American*
CDN = *Chicago Daily News*
CDT = *Chicago Daily Tribune*
CEP = *Chicago Evening Post*
CH&E = *Chicago Herald and Examiner*
DIT = (Chicago) *Daily Illustrated Times*
NYT = *New York Times*
TSN = *The Sporting News*
WP = *Washington Post*
WP&TH = *Washington Post and Times Herald*
WPTH = *Washington Post, Times Herald*

NOTES

Chapter 1

1. Violet Popovich's appearance and "stunning beauty": Mark Prescott (son of Popovich's brother Mark), telephone interview, November 13, 2012; "Bill is the boy": "Girl Who Shot Jurges Offers to Be His Bride," *CH&E*, July 8, 1932, 3; Popovich meeting Jurges: Virginia Gardner, "Jurges' Girl Friend Blames Shooting on 'Too Much Gin,'" *CDT*, July 8, 1932, 3 (includes her physical appearance); "Girl in Jurges Shooting Gives Bond," *CDN*, July 9, 1932, final edition, 3 (notes they met in 1931); "Single, running around" and Popovich seeing baseball players: Holtzman and Vass, *Baseball, Chicago Style*, 53–54.
2. Jurges family: "William Frederick Jurges," Lieske Family Tree, https://www.ancestrylibrary.com; 1920 U.S. Census, Brooklyn, New York, Enumeration District (ED) 1400, sheet no. 1-A, Frederick H. Jurges and Anna Jurges, lines 36–37, https://www.ancestrylibrary.com. Children are listed on lines 38–42: Charles, Bertha, William, Herman and Frederick. Billy Jurges: Bill Jurges, as told to Irving Vaughan, "How I Got My Start in Baseball," *CDT*, May 9, 1932, 21 (includes "maybe it was"); James J. Murphy, "Three Pals to Get Trial," *BDE*, February 6, 1927, sec. C, 6; Harold Parrott, "Billy Jurges Clicked After Boost by Pal," *BDE*, October 9, 1935, 20 (mentions Billy Gilbert and Dick Meehan); "Jurges, Boro Boy, May Report to the Cubs This Week," *BDE*, July 8, 1928, sec. C, 3; Harold C. Burr, "$100 Player Dreams of Being .400 Hitter," *BDE*, June 20, 1933,

19; Westcott, *Diamond Greats*, 100–5 (includes "in 1927"); Salin, *Baseball's Forgotten Heroes*, 159–67; Gold and Ahrens, *The Golden Era Cubs*, 144–47; Paul Geisler Jr., "Billy Jurges," SABR Baseball Biography Project, Society for American Baseball Research, https://sabr.org/bioproj/person; William Frederick Jurges, Draft Card, *U.S., World War II Draft Cards Young Men, 1940–1947*, https://www.ancestrylibrary.com (includes personal characteristics).

3. Billy Jurges: "Billy Jurges: Minor L[ea]g[ue] Stats," Baseball Reference, https://www.baseball-reference.com; Jurges, Draft Card; "Jurges Most Valuable Player," *NYT*, September 11, 1928, 25; "Cubs Acquire Shortstop from New England Team," *CDT*, July 4, 1928, 17. "He is fast": "Jurges, Boro Boy." "Two years elapsed" and spring training: Jurges, "How I Got My Start in Baseball." "I consider Jurges": Rogers Hornsby, "5-Club Race Is Seen by Hornsby," *WP*, April 13, 1931, 11. "The fact that": Edward Burns, "Cubs Hammer Four Red Pitchers; Win, 13–1," *CDT*, May 5, 1931, 25, 27.
4. Game statistics: https://www.retrosheet.org. Jurges as shortstop and English's finger: Edward Burns, "Jurges Stars as Cub Goofs and Vets Tie, 7 to 7," *CDT*, March 12, 1931, 25; "Bill Jurges, Nobody in the Minors, Big League Success," *CDT*, June 4, 1931, 27; "Cubs Lose, 7–4; Woody English Out Until June 1," *CDT*, April 10, 1932, sec. 2, 1. "Playing brilliantly": "Bill Jurges Wounded by Girl He Rejected," *NYT*, July 7, 1932, 18. "A defensive masterpiece": "William Frederic[k] Jurges," *TSN*, May 26, 1932, 1.
5. Violet Popovich: "Note Reveals Girl Planned to Kill Jurges," *CH&E*, July 7, 1932 (two different but identically titled articles from two editions of the newspaper, one from the last metropolitan edition, pp. 1 and 3, and the other from an unknown edition, pp. 1 and 5). The phrase "confession story magazines" is in Gardner, "Jurges' Girl Friend Blames Shooting" (the magazines feature emotional first-person stories). Cubs-Dodgers games: Irving Vaughan, "3 on Base, Wilson Up: Homer Beats Cubs, 5–2," *CDT*, June 10, 1932, 23 (June 9 game); Irving Vaughan, "Dodgers Whip Cubs, 4–3," *CDT*, June 11, 1932, 17 (June 10 game); "Finn and Jurges Fined $100 Each for Fight," *WP*, June 12, 1932, 15 (includes "battle royal"). "His belligerent eagerness": Clifford Bloodgood, "'If He Could Only Hit,'" *Baseball Magazine*, December 1938, 311. "Bill talked to her": Margery Rex, "Jurges' Father Says Bill Did Not Love Girl," *CA*, July 7, 1932, 3.
6. New York quarrel, the Hotel Carlos, and the Cubs' and Violet's return to Chicago: "Crazed by Love Woman Tries to Kill Self," *CA*, July 6, 1932,

1, 5 (mentions Gudat, Barton and Cuyler); "Letter Solves the Shooting of Bill Jurges," *CDT*, July 7, 1932, 1; "Cub Star Not to Prosecute Divorcee," *CA*, July 7, 1932, 3, 7. Game logs: https://www.retrosheet.org. Popovich staying at hotel and Chicago quarrel: "Note Reveals Girl Planned to Kill Jurges," 1, 5. Casual attitude and "I'm not going": Holtzman and Vass, *Baseball, Chicago Style*, 53. Glass of water: "Girl in Jurges Shooting Gives Bond" (quotes Popovich that she used a revolver). Phone call and gun shots: "Jurges, Star Cub, Is Shot," *CDN*, July 6, 1932, final edition, 1 (mentions a .32-caliber revolver); "Bill Jurges Wounded by Girl He Rejected," *NYT*, July 7, 1932, 18. The entryway floor of the six-story Hotel Carlos was partially below ground level; residents came in and walked down a set of stairs.

7. Ballplayer quotations and John Davis: "Jurges, Star Cubs, Is Shot," *CDN*, July 6, 1932, final edition, 1, 18. "Bleeding": Holtzman and Vass, *Baseball, Chicago Style*, 54. Popovich questioned: "Note Reveals Girl Planned to Kill Jurges," 3. Popovich at Bridewell: "Charge Violet with Attempt to Kill Jurges," *CH&E*, July 8, 1932, last metropolitan edition, 7. The prison was officially called the Chicago House of Corrections.

Chapter 2

8. "Bill Jurges Shot by Spurned Cabaret Girl": *DIT*, July 6, 1932, 1. "In a scuffle" and stage name: "Jurges, Star Cub, Is Shot," *CDN*, July 6, 1932, final edition, 1, 18. "A woman scorned": Associated Press, "Bill Jurges Wounded by Girl He Rejected," *NYT*, July 7, 1932, 18. Margaret Heindl: "Note Reveals Girl Planned to Kill Jurges," *CH&E*, July 7, 1932, last metropolitan edition, 3. Tony Stenella: Kay Hall, "'I Didn't Want to Kill Bill—Just Myself,' Cries Wounded Girl Who Shot Cub Star," *DIT*, July 7, 1932, 3. A search of marriage records produced no license, though perhaps the marriage was annulled. Violet's job: "William Jurges, Cubs' Shortstop, Is Shot by Girl," *CEP*, July 6, 1932, 1; "Local Ball Star Victim of Attack in Chicago Hotel," *(Forest Parkway, NY) Leader-Observer*, July 7, 1932, 1.
9. Bottles, photographs and letter: "Letter Solves the Shooting of Bill Jurges," *CDT*, July 7, 1932, 1. The letter was published in other newspapers around the country with Cuyler's first name spelled correctly.
10. "Too much gin" and "to make Bill sorry": Virginia Gardner, "Jurges' Girl Friend Blames Shooting on 'Too Much Gin,'" *CDT*, July 8, 1932,

3. "I loved him": "Cub Star Wounded by Scorned Woman," *WP*, July 7, 1932, 3. "I'm lucky": Hall, "'I Didn't Want to Kill Bill.'"

11. "Billy Darling": "Cub Star Not to Prosecute Divorcee," *CA*, July 7, 1932, 3, 7. Jurges's reply and "chestnut haired divorcée": Gardner, "Jurges' Girl Friend Blames Shooting." Photograph of upbeat Jurges: *DIT*, July 6, 1932, 1. Jurges not pressing charges and Popovich arraignment: "Charge Violet with Attempt to Kill Jurges," *CH&E*, July 8, 1932, last metropolitan edition, 7. "I understand," head shaking, "gee, I don't see," and "now famous Hotel Carlos": "Jurges Must Accuse Girl, Says Court," *CA*, July 8, 1932, 3. Jurges's parents: Margery Rex, "Jurges' Father Says Bill Did Not Love Girl," *CA*, July 7, 1932, 3. Popovich photograph and "Violet dislikes cameras": *DIT*, July 6, 1932, 3. References to Popovich: "Girl in Jurges Shooting Gives Bond," *CDN*, July 9, 1932, final edition, 3 (includes a Popovich interview and "dark-haired former"); "Jurges, Star Cub, Is Shot," 1 (includes "21-year-old comely"); picture caption, *DIT*, July 10, 1932, 1 (includes "pretty gun-toter"); "Cabaret Girl Shoots Bill Jurges, Cubs' Star Shortstop, and Self," *DIT*, July 6, 1932, 3 (includes "spurned sweetheart").

12. Biographical details and Kiki Cuyler: "Cub Star Not to Prosecute Divorcee," 3, 7 (includes *CA* quotations); "Charge Violet with Attempt to Kill Jurges" (notes *Vanities* engagement). Ned Wayburn's studio: "Ned Wayburn, Noted Follies Producer, Opens Dancing Studio in Chicago," *CDT*, November 10, 1929, Picture sec., part 2, 7. "I called him": "Girl in Jurges Shooting Gives Bond."

13. "A good girl": "Cub Star Not to Prosecute Divorcee," 3. Jurges's friend Steadman: Associated Press, "Jurges, Cub Shortstop, Shot by Scorned Woman," University of Illinois *Daily Illini*, July 7, 1932, 1. Cuyler: "Girl in Jurges Shooting Gives Bond"; "Charge Violet with Attempt to Kill Jurges" (includes "Miss Valli's charge"). Popovich dating ballplayers: Holtzman and Vass, *Baseball, Chicago Style*, 54 (includes "a big ladies' man"); Wolf, *The Called Shot*, 107 (mentions Al Lopez and Leo Durocher); "Cabaret Girl Shoots Bill Jurges," 3 (mentions Durocher); Mark Prescott, telephone interview, November 13, 2012. "Angered husbands": Jeffrey Marlett, "Leo Durocher," SABR Baseball Biography Project, Society for American Baseball Research, https://sabr.org/bioproj/person.

14. "I took the rap": Holtzman and Vass, *Baseball, Chicago Style*, 54. "Get Jurges" and target shooting: "Cabaret Girl Shoots Bill Jurges," 3. Popovich talking to Cub players: "Bill Jurges Shot by Spurned Cabaret Girl": *DIT*, July 6, 1932, 3. Jurges aware of threats, telegram and "if he denies this":

"Note Reveals Girl Planned to Kill Jurges," *CH&E*, July 7, 1932, two different but identically titled articles from two editions of the newspaper: one from the last metropolitan edition, p. 3 (includes Jurges aware of threats and "if he denies this"), and the other from an unknown edition, p. 1 (includes telegram). See also Ehrgott, *Mr. Wrigley's Ball Club*, 286–88.

15. Popovich posting bond and wanting to see Jurges: "Girl Who Shot Jurges Is Freed on $5,000 [*sic*] Bond," *CDT*, July 10, 1932, 3; "Jurges Shooting Girl Free on Bail," *DIT*, July 10, 1932, 5 (includes "from her voice"); "Girl Through A-Gunnin' for Her Star," *CA*, July 11, 1932, 3 (mentions Jurges's physician and friends). Minister's assistance and hospital: "Violet Seeks Pastor's Help to Win Jurges," *CH&E*, July 11, 1932, last metropolitan edition, 3. Radio: "Cabaret Girl Shoots Bill Jurges," 4; "Cub Star Not to Prosecute Divorcee," 7. William Veeck: "Girl Who Shot Jurges Held on Police Charge," *CDN*, July 7, 1932, final edition, 3. "Jurges unquestionably": "Cub Star Wounded by Scorned Woman." Jurges watching game: "Bill Jurges Out of Hospital; Sees Cubs Beat Braves," *CDT*, July 11, 1932, 19. Game logs: https://www.retrosheet.org.

16. Jurges working out: "Billy Jurges Back in Uniform," *CH&E*, July 14, 1932, final edition, 11. "Hope to get back": "Bill Jurges Is Better," *(Spokane, WA) Spokesman-Review*, July 15, 1932, 13. Subpoena: "Woman Who Shot Jurges to Have Hearing Today," *CDT*, July 15, 1932, 10. "She sat near": "Warneke Out for No. 13 Today," *CDT*, July 15, 1932, 22. Sbarbaro as Cubs fan: "Girl Who Shot Cub Ball Player Asks Arrest of Agent," *CEP*, August 12, 1932, 1; Ehrgott, *Mr. Wrigley's Ball Club*, 289. Bombing: "Three Bombed; One a Judge," *CDT*, February 18, 1928, 1 (includes "heavy punishment"); Eig, *Get Capone*, 48 (includes "on the take); Bergreen, *Capone*, 278 (mentions disbelief).

17. Jurges's tie and testimony, Popovich's hat and belt, "let it be recorded," and press room: "Girl Who Shot Bill Jurges Set Free by Court," *CDN*, July 15, 1932, final edition, 1, 3. Showgirls in courtroom, "Violet, a symphony," "twisted about" and Fay's testimony: "Cub Player Forgives Girl for Shooting," *DIT*, July 15, 1932, 3. "Baseball fans" and "the crowd gasped": "Jurges' Plea Frees Girl in Shooting," *CA*, July 15, 1932, 3. Jurges talking to Sbarbaro: Holtzman and Vass, *Baseball, Chicago Style*, 54. "I owe it to": "Girl Who Shot Cubs' Player Goes Free," *CDT*, July 16, 1932, 3.

18. Jurges and Popovich not speaking: Holtzman and Vass, *Baseball, Chicago Style*, 54. Jurges not talking about the shooting and bowling alley: Golenbock, *Wrigleyville*, 232 (includes "we ran"), 252–53; Alexander, *Rogers Hornsby*, 326n34. Bullet lodged: "Jurges Has 3d Bullet Removed,"

DIT, July 19, 1932, 22. "The celebrated revolver": "Jurges on 3d Base as Cubs, Pirates Start Big Series," *CEP*, July 22, 1932, 9. "Jurges bowed himself": Edward Burns, "Cubs Lose, 3–1," *CDT*, July 23, 1932, 9. Game logs: https://www.retrosheet.org.

Chapter 3

19. "I'm going to stay": "Jurges Silent; Violet Is Freed," *CH&E*, July 16, 1932, 4. Popovich and her mother: "Cub Player Forgives Girl for Shooting," *DIT*, July 15, 1932, 3. Cubs and leaflets: Edward Burns, "Five Wild Weeks Give the Cubs a Succession of Varied Thrills," *TSN*, August 18, 1932, 1. Text of leaflet: Lloyd Lewis, "Violet True to Her Name in Debut on Burlesque," *CDN*, final edition, July 27, 1932, 23.
20. Burlesque: Schiecke, *Downtown Chicago's Historic Movie Theatres*, 9–10, 167–75 (mentions area south of Van Buren Street); Corio, with DiMona, *This Was Burlesque*, 71–73 (includes Hinda Wassau story); Zeidman, *The American Burlesque Show*, 122–24, 194–95 (includes "only by exceeding"). Popovich adopting stage name: "Letter Solves the Shooting of Bill Jurges," *CDT*, July 7, 1932, 1. Popovich's show: "Amusements," *CH&E*, July 23, 1932, last metropolitan edition, 11 (includes "Bare Cub Girls"); "Amusements," *CDT*, July 26, 1932, 11 (includes "Bare Cub Follies" and "A Screamingly Funny"); Lewis, "Violet True to Her Name in Debut on Burlesque" (includes show review). Lloyd Lewis (1891–1949) was a popular Chicago newspaper columnist and a respected editor and author.
21. Burlesque show: Lloyd Lewis, "Shooter of Mr. Jurges Told Public Is Fickle," *CDN*, final edition, July 22, 1932, 25; "State-Congress Has Violet Valli as Star," *CH&E*, July 24, 1932, final home edition, sec. 3, 10; "Girl Who Shot Cub Ball Player Asks Arrest of Agent," *CEP*, August 12, 1932, 1 (mentions show performances in the past tense). "She liked to sing": Mark Prescott, telephone interview, November 16, 2015. The origin of Popovich's stage surname, Valli, is unknown.
22. Popovich seeking warrant: "Girl Who Shot Cub Ball Player Asks Arrest of Agent" (includes Barnett and Sbarbaro quotations); "Girl Who Shot Jurges Battles for His Letters," *CH&E*, August 13, 1932, 13 (includes "an affectionate nature" and injunction). Kiki Cuyler letters: "Valli 'Love' Letters Would Wreck Cubs, Accused Insists," *DIT*, August 16, 1932, 3. Popovich's lawsuit and booklet title: "Police Hold Chief of Jurges Blackmail Plot," *CDT*, August 14, 1932, sec. 2, 2.

23. Roche and Capparelli: "Nip Beer Flow to Loop from Huge Brewery," *CDT*, August 6, 1927, 1; "Policemen Kill 3 Kidnap[p]ers, Win Hero Award," *CDT*, July 17, 1932, 13. See also Ehrgott, *Mr. Wrigley's Ball Club*, 333–34. Barnett wearing glasses and "Barnett kicked": "Police Hold Chief of Jurges Blackmail Plot," sec. 2, 2–3.
24. Game logs: https://www.retrosheet.org. Lucius Barnett: "Police Hold Chief of Jurges Blackmail Plot" (includes blackmail plot and "an alleged confidence man"); "Arrest Jurges Letter Holder on Girl's Plea," *CH&E*, August 14, 1932, sec. 1, 3; "Girl Regains Jurges Notes; Continue Case," *CDT*, August 19, 1932, 23; "Valli 'Love' Letters Would Wreck Cubs," 21 (includes Barnett's comments).
25. Lucius Barnett: "Valli 'Love' Letters Would Wreck Cubs," 3, 21 (includes Barnett's comments); "Valli Letter Holder Fined; Faces Hearing," *CH&E*, August 24, 1932, 3; "Girl Regains Jurges Notes"; "Dismiss Extortion Charges in Jurges Shooting Case," *CDT*, September 9, 1932, 3. Illness of Popovich: "Jurges Letter Holder Freed," *CA*, September 8, 1932, 3. "After two months": Ehrgott, *Mr. Wrigley's Ball Club*, 347.
26. Car altercation: "She Finds Reason to Sing Blues," *CA*, March 11, 1937, 3 (includes "I insisted he let"); "Pushed from Auto," *CDT*, March 12, 1937, 18. Williams's occupation: 1930 U.S. Census, Chicago, Illinois, Enumeration District (ED) 16-184, sheet no. 39-B, Frederick B. Williams, line 52, https://www.ancestrylibrary.com. Marriage application between Fred B. Williams and Violet Popovich: *Cook County, Illinois Marriage Index, 1930–1960*, file number 1553834, https://www.ancestrylibrary.com. Popovich using her mother's name: Virginia Gardner, "Jurges' Girl Friend Blames Shooting on 'Too Much Gin,'" *CDT*, July 8, 1932, 3. Margaret Heindl: "Note Reveals Girl Planned to Kill Jurges," *CH&E*, July 7, 1932, last metropolitan edition, 3. Legal documents concerning Margaret Heindl's marriage and divorce are in the Circuit Court of Cook County Archives, Chicago, Illinois. Divorce: Margaret Popovich vs. Michael Popovich, Decree for Divorce, no. B-56160, March 30, 1920. Casual footnote: "Waitkus Shooting Recalls 1932 Jurges Incident," *WP*, June 16, 1949, 20.

Chapter 4

27. Legal documents not cited as obtained online are from the Circuit Court of Cook County Archives, Chicago, Illinois. Ancestry and emigration of Mirko Popovic, born on April 1, 1881: *U.S., Naturalization Record Indexes*,

1791–1992, https://www.ancestrylibrary.com; U.S. Department of Labor, Declaration of Intention, no. 79198, December 6, 1917 (includes personal characteristics and notes that both he and Margaret were born in Austria); U.S. Department of Labor, Petition for Naturalization, no. 56042, September 5, 1924 (includes names and birthdates of Violet and her three brothers, though Violet's birthdate is incorrect. Fog: "Lost in New York Harbor," *WP*, January 19, 1907, 3. Marriage between Mirko S. Popovich and Margaret Heindl on June 5, 1910: *Cook County, Illinois, U.S., Marriages Index, 1871–1920*, https://www.ancestrylibrary.com. Margaret Heindl's birthday of May 10, 1891: *California, Death Index, 1940–1997*, https://www.ancestrylibrary.com. Violet Popovich's birthday and names of parents: *U.S. Social Security Applications and Claims Index, 1936–2007*, https://www.ancestrylibrary.com. Drogiro Popovich's birth and death: *Cook County, Illinois, U.S., Deaths Index, 1878–1922*, https://www.ancestrylibrary.com.

28. Mirko Popovic's name change: 1910 U.S. Census, Chicago, Illinois, Enumeration District (ED) 1020, sheet no. 12-A, Mike Popovich, line 30, https://www.ancestrylibrary.com. Signatures of the Popovich children showing names of Mike Popovich, Violet Popovich, Mark Popovich, and Melvin Parker: Probate Court of Cook County, In the Matter of the Estate of Mike Popovich, Deceased: Vouchers, document 445, page 443, no. 45 P 7555, stamped July 16, 1947, Circuit Court of Cook County Archives. Mark Popovich name change to Mark Prescott: *California, U.S., County Birth, Marriage, and Death Records, 1849–1980*, https://www.ancestrylibrary.com. Melvin Parker changing his name to Melvin Parker Popovich: "Order to Show Cause," *Van Nuys (CA) News and Green Sheet*, May 19, 1972. Michael Popovich changed his last name to Prescott and had a son, Michael Prescott, as per emails from Mark Prescott (son of Violet's brother Mark), November 13, 2012 and June 16, 2016.

29. Legal documents are from the Circuit Court of Cook County Archives. "In constant fear": Margaret Popovich vs. Michael Popovich, Bill for Divorce, no. B-56160, September 3, 1919. "At that time" and Violet's testimony: Margaret Popovich vs. Michael Popovich, Certificate of Evidence, no. B-56160, March 26, 1920.

30. Legal documents are from the Circuit Court of Cook County Archives. Divorce: Margaret Popovich vs. Michael Popovich, Decree for Divorce, no. B-56160, March 30, 1920 (includes "extreme and repeated" and "as alimony for"). Michael's occupation, salary, and children: Margaret Popovich vs. Michael Popovich, Certificate of Evidence. Lack of alimony

and "unable to support": Margaret Popovich vs. Michael Popovich, Petition for Rule to Show Cause, no. B-56160, July 26, 1920. Margaret's occupation: 1920 U.S. Census, Chicago, Illinois, Enumeration District (ED) 1256, sheet no. 7-B, Margaret Popovich, line 54, https://www.ancestrylibrary.com. (All family members are listed, with places of birth, on lines 53–58.)

31. Legal documents are from the Circuit Court of Cook County Archives. Uhlich's history: "100 Years Pass for St. Paul's Evangelical," *CDT*, October 31, 1943, sec. 3, 1; "Church Looks Ahead; Marks 110 Yrs. Today," *CDT*, November 8, 1953, sec. 3, 8. Violet singing in choir: "Violet Seeks Pastor's Help to Win Jurges," *CH&E*, July 11, 1932, last metropolitan edition, 3. "A fine young": "Violet Valli Freed on Bail," *CH&E*, July 10, 1932, metropolitan edition, 3. Four Popovich children placed in Uhlich in 1920 and the three boys living there in 1922 and 1923: Margaret Popovich vs. Mike Popovich, Petition, no. B-56160, June 27, 1922; Margaret Popovich vs. Mike Popovich, Notice-Petition and Affidavit to Petition, no. B-56160, February 8, 1923. "After we had" and young Mike calling Uhlich his home: Henry W. King, Report of Superintendent to Board of Trustees, April 12, 1928, Uhlich Children's Home Records, series 1, box 1, folder 2, Chicago History Museum (see also King's report of May 10, 1928 and June 14, 1928). Mike left the orphanage on January 30, 1932; Malosh [*sic*] and Mark left on June 18, 1932. See Roll Call Ledger: Boys' Division, 1931–1932, Uhlich Records, series 1, box 3, folder 4. Violet setting the fire: Mark Prescott, telephone interview, November 13, 2012. Violet leaving Uhlich in March 1926: Minutes of the Meeting of the Board of Trustees, March 11, 1926, Uhlich Records, series 1, box 1, folder 1. "Whipped for going": "Whipped for Staying Out Late, Girl Runs Away," *CDT*, July 21, 1926, 3.

32. Violet's marriage and divorce: "Cub Star Not to Prosecute Divorcee." *CA*, July 7, 1932, 7. Violet in the chorus of *Vanities*: Virginia Gardner, "Jurges' Girl Friend Blames Shooting on 'Too Much Gin,'" *CDT*, July 8, 1932, 3. Violet as a showgirl in Chicago: "Note Reveals Girl Planned to Kill Jurges," *CH&E*, July 7, 1932, last metropolitan edition, 3. Chicago *Vanities*: "Theater," *CDT*, January 3, 1930, 15; "Theater," *CDT*, January 15, 1930, 31 (includes plot of "The Caledonian Express"); advertisement, *Playgoer* (Chicago, Illinois), January 20, 1930, 29 (notes that the Chicago show was the "original" New York production). See also "Coming Attractions," *WP*, December 1, 1929, sec. 4, 3 (includes "succeed each other" and number of people in theater company); Rubin, *Showstoppers*,

51–52, 53, 220 (includes "the most beautiful" and mentions airplane skit and concluding act). The theater program notes that there are twenty-nine scenes in the first act and eighteen scenes in the second act. Violet's name does not appear in the theater playbill, but *Vanities* playbills list only the principal performers. The eighth edition of *Vanities* came to Chicago in November 1931. See "First Nights: New Bills on Chicago Stage," *CDT*, November 15, 1931, sec. 7, 13.

33. "Mysterious girl friend": "Crazed by Love Woman Tries to Kill Self," *CA*, July 6, 1932, 5. "Girl chum": "Cabaret Girl Shoots Bill Jurges, Cubs' Star Shortstop, and Self," *DIT*, July 6, 1932, 3. "Mysterious blond companion" and Violet's mother: "Note Reveals Girl Planned to Kill Jurges," 1, 3.

34. Details about Anna Sopcak, her marriage to Michael Popovich, and Anna's daughter Betty are in the extensive testimonies in Anna Popovich vs. Michael Popovich, no. B-175582, decree entered January 14, 1930, Circuit Court of Cook County Archives. See especially testimony by Anna Popovich (pp. 2–69), testimony by Michael Popovich (pp. 75–159), and testimony by Betty Carlan, aka Betty Subject (pp. 907–25; Betty having Michael Popovich arrested is on page 918). "He kicked my mother": [Anna] Popovich vs. [Michael] Popovich, Certificate of Evidence, no. 511480, February 27, 1930, Superior Court of Cook County Archives, Chicago, Illinois. Actress Betty Subject: "Here's a 'Pleasant Subject' in Movies," *(Chicago) Day Book*, April 19, 1915, [15].

35. Details about the life of Betty Subject: "Cruelty Alleged by Wife in Suit," *San Francisco Chronicle*, November 29, 1923 (includes "frequently became"); "September Morn out of Luck in Winter of San Francisco," *Modesto (CA) Evening News*, January 5, 1924. Violet and Betty going to New York to seek employment on the stage: "Crazed by Love Woman Tries to Kill Self," *CA*, July 6, 1932, 5; "Cub Star Not to Prosecute Divorcee," *CA*, July 7, 1932, 7. "Betty is the troublemaker": Christina A. Reynen, email message, October 20, 2015. Betty E. Carlan (1896–1970), Eugene S. Carlan (1875–1945), Evelyn Subject (1893–1975), and Harold Aldine Powell (1916–1978): *California Death Index, 1940–1997*, https://www.ancestrylibrary.com.

Chapter 5

36. Chicago Cubs: James Crusinberry, "Armour, Wrigley and Banker Cub Stockholders," *CDT*, January 16, 1916, sec. 3, 1; James Crusinberry,

"Weeghman Owns Cubs," *CDT*, January 21, 1916, 11; William Wrigley Jr., "Owning a Big-League Ball Team," *Saturday Evening Post*, September 13, 1930, 24–25, 129–30. Wrigley as a major stockholder and fan: James Crusinberry, "Killefer Wagers Ten Cent Cigar," *CDT*, September 8, 1918, sec. 2, 5. "The Cubs drifted": Snyder, *Cubs Journal*, 208. Joe McCarthy: "Wrigley to Spend $1,000,000 on Cubs," *NYT*, October 14, 1925, 21. Game logs and team standings: https://www.retrosheet.org; https://www.baseball-reference.com.

37. Rogers Hornsby: Irving Vaughan, "Cubs Buy Hornsby," *CDT*, November 8, 1928, 23; "Rogers Hornsby," National Baseball Hall of Fame, https://baseballhall.org/hall-of-famers/hornsby-rogers; Associated Press, "Hornsby Clinches 7th League Batting Crown," *WP*, September 28, 1928, 13. "The addition of": James S. Collins, "Almost the Naked Truth," *WP*, April 1, 1929, 14. Game logs, statistics, and World Series games: https://www.retrosheet.org. William Wrigley's disappointment: "Hornsby Named Manager of Cubs for '31," *WP*, September 24, 1930, 13.

38. Pennant prediction and "20 per cent": "Cubs' Chiefs Again See Pennant," *WP*, March 5, 1930, 16. Game logs: https://www.retrosheet.org. Wrigley blaming McCarthy: Golenbock, *Wrigleyville*, 225. "I realize that": "Hornsby Named Manager of Cubs for '31," *WP*, September 24, 1930, 13, 16.

39. "The move may not": Irving Vaughan, "Hornsby Gets Job: Wrigley," *CDT*, September 23, 1930, 1. William Veeck Sr.: James Crusinberry, "Mitchell, Veeck, and Seys Named to Direct Cubs," *CDT*, December 8, 1918, sec. 2, 5; "Mitchell Resigns as Cub President; Veeck Is Advanced," *CDT*, July 7, 1919, 14; Jack Bales, "Baseball's First Bill Veeck," *Baseball Research Journal* 42, no. 2 (Fall 2013): 7–16. "Over my father's": Veeck with Linn, *Veeck—As in Wreck*, 25.

40. McCarthy and Hornsby: William E. Brandt, "McCarthy Is Signed as Yankee Manager," *NYT*, October 15, 1930, 27; "Hornsby Assumes Direction of Cubs," *NYT*, September 26, 1930, 30. Game logs and statistics: http://www.baseball-reference.com; https://www.retrosheet.org. Hornsby and Veeck: Edward Burns, "Hornsby Removed by Cubs," *CDT*, August 3, 1932, 1; Irving Vaughan, "Hornsby Tells of Incidents in Ouster by Cubs," *CDT*, August 6, 1932, 13; Irving Vaughan, "Veeck's Split-Up with Hornsby Blamed on 'Rear Seat Driving,'" *TSN*, August 11, 1932, 1 (includes "after that it"). "He was a very": Honig, *The Man in the Dugout*, 245.

41. Game logs: https://www.retrosheet.org. Grimm replacing Hornsby: "Hornsby Removed by Cubs," 1. Hornsby and gambling: Edward Burns,

"Five Wild Weeks Give the Cubs a Succession of Varied Thrills," *TSN*, August 18, 1932, 1, 5 (mentions "players panicky about money" owed them); Edward Burns, "Grimm Names Woody English Cubs' Captain," *CDT*, August 4, 1932, 15; "Veeck Sees No Need of Clearing Honest Players," *CDT*, August 14, 1932, sec. 2, 2 (mentions Veeck's determination to fire Hornsby); "Landis Comes and Goes, but Says Nothing," *CDT*, August 12, 1932, 19 (includes "we made a change"); "Quiz on Betting Charges Begun at Pittsburgh," *CDN*, August 11, 1932, 1–2 (includes "sweeping inquiry"); "Race Betting by Cubs Is Probed," *WP*, August 12, 1932, 11 (mentions the *CDN* story); "President Veeck's Statement," *NYT*, August 12, 1932, 20 (includes "one of the most"); "Why Hornsby Leaves the Cubs," *Literary Digest*, August 20, 1932, 30. "Like the irresistible force": Grimm, with Prell, *Jolly Cholly's Story*, 81. Kenesaw Mountain Landis: Pietrusza, *Judge and Jury*, 316–22; Edward Burns, "Landis Quiz Uncovers Hornsby Loans," *CDT*, August 14, 1932, sec. 1, 1; sec. 2, 2 (includes hearing testimony and details on money borrowed and repaid).

42. Press believing Veeck knew about gambling: Burns, "Grimm Names Woody English Cubs' Captain"; "Landis Comes and Goes." William Wrigley's death: "William Wrigley Is Dead," *CDN*, January 26, 1932, 1, 3. "Anything Veeck does": "Wrigley Has 'Hands-Off' Policy," *NYT*, August 4, 1932, 24. See also Golenbock, *Wrigleyville*, 225–31; Hornsby, *My Kind of Baseball*, 104–7; Alexander, *Rogers Hornsby*, 63, 176–81.

43. Game logs and statistics: http://www.baseball-reference.com; https://www.retrosheet.org. Mark Koenig: "Koenig Purchased by Cubs," *CDT*, August 6, 1932, 13; "Hoyt and Koenig Go to Tigers in Trade," *NYT*, May 31, 1930, 14; Daniel Shirley, "Mark Koenig," SABR Baseball Biography Project, Society for American Baseball Research, https://sabr.org/bioproj/person; Arch Ward, "Talking It Over," *CDT*, August 31, 1932, 17 (includes Veeck wanting Koenig and "hit the first ball"). Koenig's single on August 14: Edward Burns, "Cubs Lose 2–0, 2–1 Battles to Cardinals," *CDT*, August 15, 1932, 19.

44. "He just let": Honig, *The Man in the Dugout*, 246. Game logs and statistics: https://www.retrosheet.org. "Chicago's baseball hero": Edward Burns, "Homer with 2 On, 2 Out in 9th!," *CDT*, August 21, 1932, sec. 2, 1. Cubs clinching the pennant: Edward Burns, "38,000 Cheer As Cubs' Victory Clinches Flag," *CDT*, September 21, 1932, 1, 21. "Never before was": "Cubs Defy Experts and Hard Luck to Win," *CDT*, September 21, 1932, 21. "The ball started": Grimm, *Jolly Cholly's Story*, 88. "Koenig really helped us": Golenbock, *Wrigleyville*, 233.

45. World Series shares: Edward Burns, "Cubs Split Series Money," *CDT*, September 22, 1932, 23; Irving Vaughan, "Home Field Buoys Cubs for Third Game," *CDT*, October 1, 1932, 19; "World Series Gate Receipts," Baseball Almanac, https://www.baseball-almanac.com. "We figured he wasn't": Golenbock, *Wrigleyville*, 233. "Sure, I'm on 'em": "Babe Airs His Views of Cubs and 'Chiseling,'" *CDT*, September 30, 1932, 21. See also Irving Vaughan, "Cubs' Slicing of Melon Proves Old Sores Are Still Unhealed," *TSN*, September 29, 1932, 1.
46. "The Cubs' stinginess": "Scribbled by Scribes," *TSN*, October 13, 1938, 4. World Series data: "1932 World Series," Baseball Almanac, https://www.baseball-almanac.com (includes attendance). Bleachers and game-day accounts: Edward Burns, "Home Runs by Ruth, Gehrig Beat Cubs, 7–5," *CDT*, October 2, 1932, sec. 1, 1; sec. 2, 2; John Drebinger, "Yankees Beat Cubs for 3d in Row, 7–5," *NYT*, October 2, 1932, sec. 3, 1, 9. Game logs: https://www.retrosheet.org. "I'd play for half": Creamer, *Babe*, 360. "I was playing": Golenbock, *Wrigleyville*, 234.
47. "Threw hard" and "the Yankees just had": Golenbock, *Wrigleyville*, 234. "Anybody who knows me": Creamer, *Babe*, 366–67. World Series games: https://www.retrosheet.org; "1932 World Series," Baseball Almanac. Joe Williams: Joe Williams, "Ruth Calls Shot as He Puts Homer No. 2 in Side Pocket," *New York World-Telegram*, October 1, 1932, Sports sec., 6. Game day accounts and eyewitness reports: Ehrgott, *Mr. Wrigley's Ball Club*, 451–55; Sherman, *Babe Ruth's Called Shot*, 99–113.
48. "I thought he": Sherman, *Babe Ruth's Called Shot*, 108. "Definitely pointed": Ray Canton, "Pat Pieper of the Cubs," *CDT Magazine*, August 30, 1953, 12. "And that Ruth": Daniel M. Daniel, "Rambling Round the Circuit with Pitcher Snorter Casey," *TSN*, December 22, 1932, 6. "The Babe actually": Grimm, *Jolly Cholly's Story*, 90. "Pointed to the dugout" and "I may be dumb": Golenbock, *Wrigleyville*, 236, 238–39. Gehrig, Gomez, Pipgras, and Sewell: Rubenstein, *Chicago in the World Series, 1903–2005*, 131. Crosetti: Anthony McCarron, "Crosetti Makes Point on Babe," *New York Daily News*, May 18, 2001, 81. McCarthy: Honig, *The Man in the Dugout*, 86–87. "All of us players": Povich, *All These Mornings*, 50.
49. "He called shots": Montville, *The Big Bam*, 312. "A great guy": Golenbock, *Wrigleyville*, 236. "Had just witnessed": Drebinger, "Yankees Beat Cubs for 3d in Row, 7–5." Charlie Root and the Called Shot: Snell, *Root for the Cubs*, 238–39, 244–45, 253. Game logs and statistics: https://www.retrosheet.org; https://www.baseball-almanac.com. Art Ahrens: Ahrens, *Chicago Cubs, 1926–1940*, 36.

50. Jurges and Koenig statistics: "1932 World Series," Baseball Almanac. "Bullet Bill Jurges": "Bill Jurges Leads N. L. Shortstops," *CDT*, December 28, 1932, 17. Game logs and statistics: https://www.retrosheet.org. Koenig's wrist: "Koenig Injures Wrist, May Not Play Today," *WP*, September 29, 1932, 11. "I never fit in": Shirley, "Mark Koenig." Koenig traded: Edward Burns, "Cubs Get Chuck Klein for Cash, 3 Players," *CDT*, November 22, 1933, 21.
51. The Cubs' votes: Irving Vaughan, "Cubs Battle Yankees," *CDT*, September 28, 1932, 19; Vaughan, "Cubs' Slicing of Melon," 1 (mentions fans' letters). Commissioner Landis meeting: Golenbock, *Wrigleyville*, 233. "Never will be equaled": Edward Burns, "Fine Baseball Year—If You'll Forget Series," *CDT*, December 25, 1932, sec. 2, 1.
52. "I guess I'll remain": "Jurges Must Accuse Girl, Says Court," *CA*, July 8, 1932, 3. Mary Elizabeth Reinhart Huyett: *Pennsylvania, U.S., Birth Certificates, 1906–1911*, https://www.ancestrylibrary.com; "William Frederick Jurges," Lieske Family Tree, https://www.ancestrylibrary.com. Marriage and games on wedding day: Edward Burns, "Cubs Idle; Buy Wedding Gifts for Jurges," *CDT*, June 28, 1933, 25; "Inspiration," *WP*, June 29, 1933, 15; "Cubs Conquer Phils Twice, 9–5 and 8–3," *NYT*, June 29, 1933, 24.

Chapter 6

53. Game logs and team standings: https://www.retrosheet.org. Jurges's appendicitis: "Operate Today on Bill Jurges for Appendicitis," *CDT*, June 28, 1934, 21; "Braves Down Cubs; Klein, Jurges Back," *WP*, August 18, 1934, 15. Jurges's daughter: "Bill Jurges, Cub Shortstop, Becomes Father of Girl," *CDT*, April 24, 1934, 23; Edward Burns, "Jurges Signs," *CDT*, January 31, 1935, 19.
54. Unemployment: Mead, *Low and Outside*, 45 (includes Landis quotation); Ehrgott, *Mr. Wrigley's Ball Club*, 264 (mentions Chicago's unemployment). Salary and roster cuts: Associated Press, "Salary Lists of Major Leagues to Be Cut $1,000,000 This Year," *NYT*, January 13, 1932, 28. Baseball attendance: Robert L. Tiemann, "Major League Attendance," in Thorn and others, *Total Baseball*, 76. Salaries: Voigt, *Baseball*, 174. See also Alexander, *Breaking the Slump*, 36–78. "Foresees nothing": Burns, "Jurges Signs."
55. "A perfect day": "Jurges Leads in 14 Hit Attack on Pirate Hurlers," *CDT*, July 8, 1935, 17. Game logs, team standings, and World Series games: https://www.retrosheet.org. "Broke out like big": George Estep, "Way

We Were," *Chicago Tribune Magazine*, April 13, 1986, 11. "Eleven in a row": Irving Vaughan, "Cubs Take First Place," *CDT*, September 15, 1935, sec. 2, 3. Clinching the pennant: "Cubs Clinch Pennant," *NYT*, September 28, 1935, 1.

56. "Abominable behavior": Stout and Johnson, *The Cubs*, 163. "Both clubs had great": Grimm, with Prell, *Jolly Cholly's Story*, 112.

57. Greenberg and Cavarretta quotations: Greenberg, *Hank Greenberg*, 82–83. "I never have" and Cubs ejections: Edward Burns, "Landis Investigates Cub Feud with Umpire," *CDT*, October 5, 1935, 21, 24.

58. Landis and two teams: Associated Press, "Landis Investigates Wrangle," *NYT*, October 5, 1935, 9 (mentions meeting); "Landis Will Defer Action on Dispute," *NYT*, October 6, 1935, 73 (includes "could be heard"); "Moriarty, 4 Cubs Fined $200 for Series Row," *CDT*, October 25, 1935, 29–30 (includes fines, "vile," and "I used all"); "Greenberg Backs Moriarty," *NYT*, October 25, 1935, 27 (includes "the charges against").

59. Jurges's statistics: https://www.retrosheet.org. Jurges striking out: "Detailed Account of Deciding Game," *NYT*, October 8, 1935, 29. "No one has": Edward Burns, "Jurges Arrives at Cub Camp," *CDT*, February 26, 1936, 19. Jurges's arm: Irving Vaughan, "Jurges Out of Cub Lineup for Giants Today," *CDT*, May 2, 1936, 23; Associated Press, "Late Rallies Give Pirates Two Triumphs Over Cubs Before Crowd of 43,332," *NYT*, May 31, 1936, sec. 5, 7. Game logs and statistics: https://www.retrosheet.org. Hitting slump: Associated Press, "Baseball Season Ends," *WP*, September 28, 1936, 16. "Their faint hopes": Edward Burns, "Campbell Slugs Jurges as Reds Win," *CDT*, September 8, 1936, 27.

60. Game logs and statistics: https://www.retrosheet.org. August 7 game and Jurges's shoulder: Irving Vaughan, "Sore Shoulder Puts Jurges Out for a Few Days," *CDT*, August 27, 1937, 23. "My arm was caught": Westcott, *Diamond Greats*, 104. Wrigley Field renovations: Wayne K. Otto, "Touching All Bases," *CH&E*, April 18, 1938, 18; Edward Burns, "New Wrigley Field Blooms in Scenic Beauty," *CDT*, September 12, 1937, sec. 2, 5 (includes "if the truth"); Stout and Johnson, *The Cubs*, 165.

61. Jurges interview: "Jurges Speaks of Many Things, Including Cubs," *CDT*, February 12, 1938, 21. Dizzy Dean trade: Associated Press, "Chicago Paid $185,000 Cash for Dizzy Dean," *WP*, April 19, 1938, 16; Irving Vaughan, "Dizzy Dean Traded to Cubs," *CDT*, April 17, 1938, sec. 2, 1, 3 (includes Grimm quotations); "Dizzy Trade," *Time*, April 25, 1938, 52.

62. Game logs and statistics: https://www.retrosheet.org. Games: Irving Vaughan, "Dizzy Yields Eight Hits in Six Innings," *CDT*, April 21, 1938,

21 (April 20 game); Irving Vaughan, "Dean and Cubs Whip Cards, 5–0," *CDT*, April 25, 1938, 17 (April 24 game); "Dean Will Be Idle at Least a Month," *NYT*, May 5, 1938, 29 (includes "ordered to rest"); Associated Press, "Dean, in Brilliant Return, Beats Bees, 3–1, as Cubs Win Twin Bill," *NYT*, July 18, 1938, 16 (July 17 game).

63. Fading pennant hopes: Associated Press, "Dean, in Brilliant Return." Phil Cavarretta: Golenbock, *Wrigleyville*, 259. Charlie Grimm's failings: Bartell, with Macht, *Rowdy Richard*, 215. "Charlie Grimm has done": Associated Press, "'Change Is Necessary,' Says Owner," *WP*, July 21, 1938, 19. Statistics and team standings: https://www.retrosheet.org. "To a generation": Shirley Povich, "This Morning," *WP*, July 21, 1938, 19.

64. Game logs and team standings: https://www.retrosheet.org. Gabby Hartnett's debut: Irving Vaughan, "Cubs Win and Lose in Hartnett's Debut," *CDT*, July 22, 1938, 19, 21. Dick Bartell: Bartell, *Rowdy Richard*, 205. "The Jurges-Bartell imbroglio": Irving Vaughan, "Cubs Whip Giants, 7–4, 3–1, Before 43,233," *CDT*, July 24, 1938, sec. 2, 1. "September World Series" and "thrills never abated": Edward Burns, "Cubs Whip Pirates, 2–1," *CDT*, September 28, 1938, 21. "I wasn't going": Associated Press, "Mates Cheer Dizzy Dean," *WP*, September 28, 1938, 18.

65. The 34,465 fans and *Tribune* quotations: Edward Burns, "Hartnett Hits Homer in Ninth," *CDT*, September 29, 1938, 1, 22. Tired Cubs pitchers and "the two greatest": Associated Press, "Circuit Slap in 9th Ends 5-to-5 Tie," *WP*, September 29, 1938, 21. "The crowd was": Ritter, *The Glory of Their Times*, 343. "We surrender": John P. Carmichael, "The Barber Shop," *CDN*, September 29, 1938, 27.

66. "That home run": Ritter, *The Glory of Their Times*, 344. Cubs clinching the pennant: Edward Burns, "Cubs Win; Now for Yankees!," *CDT*, October 2, 1938, sec. 1, 1; sec. 2, 4. Game logs, team standings, and World Series games: https://www.retrosheet.org. Cubs swept in World Series: Irving Vaughan, "Yankees Crush Cubs, 8 to 3," *CDT*, October 10, 1938, 19–20.

67. "There'll be a clean": "Cub Leader Plans Drastic Shake-Up," *NYT*, October 11, 1938, 29. Wrigley job offer, "Mr. Wrigley," and "the first trade": George Strickler, "In the Wake of the News," *CDT*, July 4, 1959, sec. 2, 1. Jurges trade: "Three Cubs Traded for Three Giants," *CDT*, December 7, 1938, 25, 27. Jurges a possible threat to Hartnett: Phalen, *Our Chicago Cubs*, 4. "We all talked": Golenbock, *Wrigleyville*, 265. Jurges living close to home: J. G. Taylor Spink, "Looping the Loops," *TSN*, December 15, 1948, 4. "I think the change": John Drebinger, "Giants Begin Work in Louisiana Camp," *NYT*, March 6, 1939, 20.

68. "This Spring he": John Drebinger, "Trade Aids Giants," *NYT*, March 21, 1939, 34. "Billy Jurges, closing": John Drebinger, "Warneke Shelled by Giant Bats, 6–3," *NYT*, May 5, 1939, 33. Game logs and statistics: https://www.retrosheet.org. Jurges's injury: "Jurges, Williams, Bowman Hurt in Baseball Mishaps," *CDT*, June 24, 1940, 19, 21; "Miller Replaces Jurges," *NYT*, July 6, 1940, 10 (mentions All-Star Game); John Drebinger, "Jurges Needs No Operation Now," *NYT*, February 14, 1941, 21; "Bill Jurges Back in Giants' Line-up," *WP*, March 31, 1941, 18. All-Star Games: "Billy Jurges," Baseball Reference, https://www.baseball-reference.com. Batting helmets: Frederick G. Lieb, "Leagues Take Action on Helmets," *TSN*, July 11, 1940, 1; "Giants Test Helmets Today," *NYT*, May 9, 1941, 26.
69. "Giants Release Jurges," *NYT*, November 8, 1945, 27; "Jurges Signs with Braves," *NYT*, December 6, 1945, 39; "Butcher, Jurges Out," *WP*, March 22, 1946, 12; "Bill Jurges to Rejoin Cubs for Utility Infield Duty," *CDT*, March 24, 1946, sec. 2, 1. "I was happy": Phalen, *Our Chicago Cubs*, 3.
70. Jurges working for Cubs: Irving Vaughan, "Cubs Decide Bill Jurges Is a Coach Again," *CDT*, October 22, 1946, 23; Milt Woodard, "Jurges, at 39, Reactivated as Cub Shortstop," *TSN*, September 3, 1947, 11. Jurges's last game: https://www.retrosheet.org. Jurges leaving the Cubs: "Cubs' Session for Farm Clubs," *CDT*, October 23, 1948, sec. 2, 2. Spalding firm and quotations: Spink, "Looping the Loops."
71. The Indians' farm club: "Three-Eye Will Open Today," *CDT*, April 23, 1950, sec. A, 6; "Cedar Rapids Drops Jurges," *NYT*, October 14, 1950, 26; Jack Lang, "Jurges Seeks Dodger Coaching Job," *TSN*, December 6, 1950, 20 (mentions Indians). Government job: untitled paragraph, *TSN*, May 14, 1952, 23; Bob Addie, "Bill Owes 'It All to Cookie,'" *TSN*, July 15, 1959, 3. Boston Braves: "Braves Make Jurges Coach," *WP*, February 10, 1952, sec. 3, 2; "Jurges Leaves Braves," *CDT*, March 7, 1952, sec. 4, 2; "Bunts and Boots," *TSN*, March 19, 1952, 28. Hagerstown Braves: "Harassed Hagerstown Owner Names Bill Jurges Manager," *WP*, July 12, 1953, sec. 3, 2; "Pilot Jurges Victor in Debut," *TSN*, July 22, 1953, 34; "Senators' Third-Base Coach Steps into Job," *WP&TH*, July 4, 1959, sec. A, 10 (mentions second-place Braves). "It's strange": Dick Young, "Clubhouse Confidential," *TSN*, December 22, 1954, 16.
72. "I've spent every year": George Strickler, "In the Wake of the News," *CDT*, July 4, 1959, sec. 2, 1. "In the majors": Spink, "Looping the Loops." Game logs and team standings: https://www.retrosheet.org. Jurges wanting to manage: "Higgins Out; Jurges Red Sox Pilot," *NYT*, July 4,

1959, 10. Firing of Higgins: Hy Hurwitz, "Higgins Dropped as Red Sox Pilot—Jurges Named," *TSN*, July 8, 1959, 16. Jurges's contract: "Senators' Third-Base Coach Steps into Job When Higgins Is Fired," *WP&TH*, July 4, 1959, sec. A, 8. Jurges catching a plane: "Jurges Excited," *CDT*, July 4, 1959, sec. 2, 1. The Orioles' victory and Ted Williams: "Orioles Send Red Sox to 7th Loss in Row," *NYT*, July 5, 1959, sec. 5, 3.

73. July 4 and July 5 games: Hy Hurwitz, "Defeat Mars Bill's Bow," *TSN*, July 15, 1959, 5. Game logs, team standings, and managerial records: https://www.retrosheet.org. Air of complacency: Jack Mann, "The Great Wall of Boston," *Sports Illustrated*, June 28, 1965, 46, 51. July 24 article: Ed Rumill, "Don't Care Slant Seen in Red Sox," *Christian Science Monitor*, July 24, 1959, Atlantic edition, 1. Jackie Jensen: Bob Addie, "Bob Addie's Column," *WP&TH*, July 29, 1959, sec. C, 3. "I challenge the player": "Challenge from Jurges to Team Gets No Takers," *CDT*, July 26, 1959, sec. 2, 2. Pumpsie Green and injured players: "White Sox Score Over Boston, 2–1," *NYT*, July 22, 1959, 31; Associated Press, "Sox Problems Remain; Overshadow Additions," *Christian Science Monitor*, July 24, 1959, Atlantic edition, 15. "Superior": Shirley Povich, "This Morning," *WPTH*, June 14, 1960, sec. A, 18.

74. Williams and Jensen: "Williams' Ailment Can Cost Red Sox $1,000 Every Day," *NYT*, April 1, 1959, 45; Edward Prell, "Jackie Gone, Ted Going," *CDT*, February 10, 1960, sec. 4, 1; "Jensen Quits Baseball," *WPTH*, January 27, 1960, sec. C, 1. Game logs and player records: https://www.retrosheet.org. "I'm quite concerned": Hy Hurwitz, "Juggling Jurges May Give Clinton Whirl in Outfield," *TSN*, April 6, 1960, 22. "Hit the ceiling" and "a big leaguer makes": Hy Hurwitz, "Tom Sturdivant Steps to Front as Stopper," *TSN*, April 13, 1960, 17. Pro-Mike Higgins faction: Jerry Nason, "Unlovely Truth: Red Sox Are Terrible," *Boston Globe*, April 27, 1960, evening edition, 51. "Tremendous desire": Bob Holbrook, "Players Mum; Jurges' Move Next," *Boston Globe*, April 26, 1960, evening edition, 51.

75. April 26 meeting and quotations: Joe Reichler, "Ted Backs Manager," *Boston Globe*, April 27, 1969, morning edition, 35, 41. See also Roger Birtwell, "Jurges Defends Strategy," *Boston Globe*, April 26, 1960, morning edition, 41–42. "Pal" and "the Red Sox started": Nason, "Unlovely Truth."

76. Critics silenced: Arthur Siegel, "Nieder Fingers Burglar's Grip," *Boston Globe*, April 27, 1960, evening edition, 51. April 26 game, clubhouse meeting, and quotations: Bob Holbrook, "Sox Furor Calms After Meeting,"

Boston Globe, April 27, 1960, evening edition, 51–52. Game logs and team standings: https://www.retrosheet.org. "Hustling and giving" and "you couldn't blame": Ed Rumill, "Buddin Leads Boston out of Hitting Slump," *Christian Science Monitor*, May 26, 1960, Atlantic edition, 16.

77. Game logs and team standings: https://www.retrosheet.org. "I don't think": Bob Addie, "Bob Addie's Column," *WP&TH*, July 5, 1959, sec. C, 1. Jurges taking a rest: "Jurges Takes Vacation from Boston Pilot's Job," *CDT*, June 9, 1960, sec. 8, 1; Arthur Daley, "Sports of the Times," *NYT*, June 10, 1960, 23 (includes "no job is worth"); Hy Hurwitz, "Baker Takes Hub Skipper Seat as Exhaustion Benches Jurges," *TSN*, June 15, 1960, 16 (includes "completely exhausted").

78. Jurges's firing: "Bosox Make It Official: Fire Jurges," *WPTH*, June 11, 1960, 18; "Billy Says: 'Best for All,'" *WPTH*, June 11, 1960, 18. Game logs, team standings, and Jurges's managerial record: https://www.retrosheet.org. Mike Higgins rehired: "Higgins Returns to Manage Bosox," *WPTH*, June 13, 1960, sec. A, 16. "When you become": Stan Grosshandler, "Billy Jurges Recalls How It Was in Majors in 1930s," *Baseball Digest*, October 1992, 70.

79. Jurges joining teams: "Jurges Joins Orioles," *NYT*, July 4, 1960, 10; "Jurges Named Scout," *WPTH*, April 3, 1961, sec. A, 16 (Mets); "Bill Jurges Joins Houston Colts," *WPTH*, January 11, 1962, sec. A, 22. Senators and "Houston was very good": Bob Addie, "Nats Add Mullin to Coaching Staff, Hire Jurges as Major-League Scout," *WPTH*, November 15, 1968, sec. D, 1.

80. Jurges as baseball scout: Westcott, *Diamond Greats*, 104–5 (includes "all I ever"); Hy Zimmerman, "M's Banking on Draft Choice for Paciorek," *TSN*, November 25, 1978, 46 (mentions Mariners and Cubs). Eddie Mathews: Hy Hurwitz, "Braves' Mathews Tagged 'Pitcher-Killer,'" *TSN*, May 21, 1952, 5. Harmon Killebrew: Bob Addie, "Bill Owes 'It All to Cookie,'" *TSN*, July 15, 1959, 3–4. Jurges's reputation as a scout and Mary Jurges's deteriorating health: Salin, *Baseball's Forgotten Heroes*, 165.

Chapter 7

81. "No, indeed": Bob Addie, "Bill Owes 'It All to Cookie,'" *TSN*, July 15, 1959, 3. "We traveled": Bill Price, email message, November 15, 2011. Reagan and radio station: David Mervin, *Ronald Reagan and the American Presidency* (New York: Routledge, 2014), 70. "One night we": Westcott, *Diamond Greats*, 103.

82. Mary Jurges's obituary: "Deaths: Jurges, Mary Elizabeth," *WP*, March 17, 1984, sec. B, 4. "I enjoy the good life": Eddie Gold, "Ex-Cub Shortstop Billy Jurges," *Chicago Sun-Times*, April 3, 1988, 81. "Cubs, Giants, good year": J.G. Taylor Spink, "Looping the Loops," *TSN*, December 15, 1948, 4. Jurges's statistics: "Billy Jurges," Baseball Reference, https://www.baseball-reference.com. Traveling and cancer: Salin, *Baseball's Forgotten Heroes*, 165. Jurges and hospital, death, and "he was a wonderful": Phyllis Jurges, letter to "Mr. Levy," May 6, 1998, author's collection. "Although I was": Bill Price, email message, November 12, 2020. Jurges visiting with ballplayers and Suzanne Price quotations: Suzanne Price, telephone interview, September 21, 2011.
83. Los Angeles: 1940 U.S. Census, Los Angeles, California, Enumeration District (ED) 60-109, sheet no. 9-A, Margaret Heindl and Violet Heindl Popovich, lines 23–24, https://www.ancestrylibrary.com (according to the census, Violet earned no money in 1939 as a "singer, professionally"; her mother was a retired seamstress and dressmaker). Marriage between Charles Retzlaff and Violet Popovich on April 17, 1947: Minnesota Official Marriage System, certificate number 0040-323, https://moms.mn.gov. Charley Retzlaff: James P. Dawson, "Crowd of 17,000 Sees Louis Stop Retzlaff and Gain His 27th Straight Victory," *NYT*, January 18, 1936, 10. Observations about Popovich: Mark Prescott, telephone interview, November 13, 2012, and assorted email messages. "Bad reputation": Holtzman and Vass, *Baseball, Chicago Style*, 54.
84. Violet Popovich: Michael Prescott (son of Popovich's brother Michael), assorted correspondence; telephone interview, January 24, 2020; Mark Prescott, telephone interview, November 13, 2012. Violet's date of death: *U.S., Social Security Death Index, 1935–2014*, https://www.ancestrylibrary.com. Grave: Forest Lawn—Hollywood Hills, http://forestlawn.com/hollywood-hills. Violet's father's death on October 10, 1945: *Cook County, Illinois Death Index, 1908–1988*, https://www.ancestrylibrary.com. Violet's mother's death on October 15, 1957: *California, Death Index, 1940–1997*, https://www.ancestrylibrary.com.
85. Sheffield House Hotel: "Sheffield House Hotel," Yelp, https://www.yelp.com. "The place was": Ed Hartig, email message, May 3, 2020. Sheffield sold and remodeled: Kate Sosin, "Hundreds to Be Displaced as Lakeview Hotels Close," *(Chicago) Windy City Times*, August 10, 2011, http://www.windycitymediagroup.com (mentions 105 residents); Emily Badger, "What Happens When Housing for the Poor Is Remodeled as Luxury Studios," *WP*, November 12, 2014, https://www.washingtonpost.

com (mentions 130 units). "3834 N Sheffield" and "once hip apartment": "3834 N Sheffield: A Lakeview Apartment," BJB Properties, https://www.bjbproperties.com.

86. "I was very angry": Mark Prescott, telephone interview, November 13, 2012. "Collect one-night stands": Ardell, *Breaking into Baseball*, 52. "She was desperate": Ed Hartig, email message, January 6, 2016. "The shooting of Jurges": Ed Hartig, "The Original 'Wonder Boys,'" Chicago Cubs *Vine Line* 18, no. 2 (February 2003): 31 (mentions Waitkus, Jurges, and *The Natural*). "Twisted fascination": Louther S. Horne, "Baseball Star Shot by Girl Fan Rallies," *NYT*, June 16, 1949, 23. Jurges's last game: https://www.retrosheet.org. See also Rob Edelman, "Eddie Waitkus and *The Natural*: What Is Assumption? What Is Fact?," *The National Pastime* (2013): 86–91.

BIBLIOGRAPHY

Books

Ahrens, Art. *Chicago Cubs, 1926–1940*. Images of Baseball. Charleston, SC: Arcadia Publishing, 2005.

Alexander, Charles C. *Breaking the Slump: Baseball in the Depression Era*. New York: Columbia University Press, 2002.

———. *Rogers Hornsby: A Biography*. New York: Henry Holt, 1995.

Ardell, Jean Hastings. *Breaking into Baseball: Women and the National Pastime*. Carbondale: Southern Illinois University Press, 2005.

Bartell, Dick, with Norman L. Macht. *Rowdy Richard: A Firsthand Account of the National League Baseball Wars of the 1930s and the Men Who Fought Them*. Berkeley, CA: North Atlantic Books, 1987.

Bergreen, Laurence. *Capone: The Man and the Era*. New York: Simon and Schuster, 1994.

Corio, Ann, with Joseph DiMona. *This Was Burlesque*. New York: Grosset & Dunlap, 1968.

Creamer, Robert W. *Babe: The Legend Comes to Life*. 1974. Reprint, New York: Simon and Schuster, 2005.

Ehrgott, Roberts. *Mr. Wrigley's Ball Club: Chicago and the Cubs during the Jazz Age*. Lincoln: University of Nebraska Press, 2013.

Eig, Jonathan. *Get Capone: The Secret Plot That Captured America's Most Wanted Gangster*. New York: Simon and Schuster, 2010.

Gold, Eddie, and Art Ahrens. *The Golden Era Cubs, 1876–1940*. Chicago: Bonus Books, 1985.

Golenbock, Peter. *Wrigleyville: A Magical History Tour of the Chicago Cubs*. New York: St. Martin's Press, 1996.

Greenberg, Hank. *Hank Greenberg: The Story of My Life*. Edited by Ira Berkow. New York: Times Books, 1989.

Grimm, Charlie, with Ed Prell. *Jolly Cholly's Story: Baseball, I Love You!* Chicago: Henry Regnery, 1968.

Holtzman, Jerome, and George Vass. *Baseball, Chicago Style: A Tale of Two Teams, One City*. New exp. ed. Los Angeles: Bonus Books, 2005.

Honig, Donald. *The Man in the Dugout: Fifteen Big League Managers Speak Their Minds*. Chicago: Follett, 1977.

Hornsby, Rogers. *My Kind of Baseball*. Edited by J. Roy Stockton. New York: David McKay, 1953.

Mead, William B. *Low and Outside*. Alexandria, VA: Redefinition, 1990.

Montville, Leigh. *The Big Bam: The Life and Times of Babe Ruth*. New York: Broadway Books, 2006.

Phalen, Rick. *Our Chicago Cubs: Inside the History and the Mystery of Baseball's Favorite Franchise*. South Bend, IN: Diamond Communications, 1992.

Pietrusza, David. *Judge and Jury: The Life and Times of Judge Kenesaw Mountain Landis*. South Bend, IN: Diamond Communications, 1998.

Povich, Shirley. *All These Mornings*. Englewood Cliffs, NJ: Prentice-Hall, 1969.

Ritter, Lawrence S. *The Glory of Their Times: The Story of the Early Days of Baseball Told by the Men Who Played It*. Enl. ed. New York: Perennial, 2002.

Rubenstein, Bruce A. *Chicago in the World Series, 1903–2005: The Cubs and White Sox in Championship Play*. Jefferson, NC: McFarland, 2006.

Rubin, Martin. *Showstoppers: Busby Berkeley and the Tradition of Spectacle*. New York: Columbia University Press, 1993.

Salin, Tony. *Baseball's Forgotten Heroes: One Fan's Search for the Game's Most Interesting Overlooked Players*. Lincolnwood, IL: Masters Press, 1999.

Schiecke, Konrad. *Downtown Chicago's Historic Movie Theatres*. Jefferson, NC: McFarland, 2012.

Sherman, Ed. *Babe Ruth's Called Shot: The Myth and Mystery of Baseball's Greatest Home Run*. Guilford, CT: Lyons Press, 2014.

Snell, Roger. *Root for the Cubs: Charlie Root and the 1929 Chicago Cubs*. Nicholasville, KY: Wind Publications, 2009.

Snyder, John. *Cubs Journal: Year by Year and Day by Day with the Chicago Cubs Since 1876*. Cincinnati: Clerisy Press, 2008.

Stout, Glenn, and Richard A. Johnson. *The Cubs: The Complete Story of Chicago Cubs Baseball*. Boston: Houghton Mifflin, 2007.

Thorn, John, and others, eds. *Total Baseball: The Official Encyclopedia of Major League Baseball*. 7th ed. Kingston, NY: Total Sports Publishing, 2001.

Veeck, Bill, with Ed Linn. *Veeck—As in Wreck: The Autobiography of Bill Veeck*. New York: G. P. Putnam's Sons, 1962.

Voigt, David Quentin. *Baseball: An Illustrated History*. University Park: Pennsylvania State University Press, 1994.

Westcott, Rich. *Diamond Greats: Profiles and Interviews with 65 of Baseball's History Makers*. Westport, CT: Meckler Books, 1988.

Wolf, Thomas. *The Called Shot: Babe Ruth, the Chicago Cubs, and the Unforgettable Major League Baseball Season of 1932*. Lincoln: University of Nebraska Press, 2020.

Zeidman, Irving. *The American Burlesque Show*. New York: Hawthorn Books, 1967.

Newspapers

Boston Globe
Brooklyn (NY) *Daily Eagle*
Chicago American
Chicago Daily News
Chicago Daily Tribune
Chicago Evening Post
Chicago Herald and Examiner
Christian Science Monitor
(Chicago) *Daily Illustrated Times*
New York Times
Washington Post
Washington Post and Times Herald
Washington Post, Times Herald

Baseball Periodical

The Sporting News

Bibliography

Archives

Chicago History Museum, Chicago, Illinois
Circuit Court of Cook County Archives, Chicago, Illinois
National Baseball Hall of Fame Library, Cooperstown, New York
Superior Court of Cook County Archives, Chicago, Illinois

Websites

Ancestry Library Edition. https://www.ancestrylibrary.com.
Baseball Almanac. https://www.baseball-almanac.com.
Baseball Reference. https://www.baseball-reference.com.
Retrosheet. https://www.retrosheet.org.
Society for American Baseball Research. https://sabr.org.

Interviews

Mark Prescott
Michael Prescott
Suzanne Price
William Price

INDEX

A

Ahrens, Art 76
American League 79, 94, 95, 97

B

Baltimore Orioles 94, 98
Barnett, Lucius 49, 51, 52
Bartell, Dick 76, 87
Barton, Vince 28, 30
BJB Properties 107
Black Sox scandal 69
Boston Braves 40, 63, 92, 93, 99
Boston Red Sox 94–98
Bridewell Prison and Hospital 32, 35, 39
Brooklyn Dodgers 26, 51, 68, 81, 83, 87, 93
Burke, James M. 41, 43
burlesque 44, 45–48
Bush, Guy 68, 69, 74

C

Carroll, Earl 37, 59
Cavarretta, Phil 79, 82, 85, 91, 102
Chicago Cubs 25, 63, 98
- 1929 season 64
- 1930 season 65, 66
- 1931 season 26, 66
- 1932 season 26–28, 40, 43–44, 67–78, 109
- 1933 season 79
- 1934 season 79
- 1935 season 81 83
- 1936 season 83
- 1937 season 84
- 1938 season 85–88, 90–92
- 1946 and 1947 seasons 92–93
- National League pennant (1929) 63
- National League pennant (1932) 67, 71, 78, 109
- National League pennant (1935) 81
- National League pennant (1938) 90

World Series (1929) 64
World Series (1932) 72–78, 109
World Series (1935) 81–83
World Series (1938) 90
Chicago Daily News 69, 72
Cincinnati Reds 26, 85, 88
Cuyler, Kiki 28, 34, 35, 37, 38, 39, 49, 51, 52, 67

D

Davis, Dr. John C. 30, 40
Dean, Dizzy 85, 86, 88
Depression (United States)
baseball attendance 79
baseball salaries 80–81
Detroit Tigers 71, 81–83
Durocher, Leo 38

E

Earl Carroll Vanities 37, 59
English, Woody 26, 42, 43, 68, 69, 72, 73, 78, 82, 83

F

Finn, Neal 27, 28

G

Gehrig, Lou 72, 73, 74, 75
Greenberg, Hank 81, 82, 83
Green, Pumpsie 95, 96, 97
Grimm, Charlie 68, 69, 71, 74, 75, 79, 81, 82, 83, 85, 86, 87, 91, 93
Gudat, Marv 28

H

Hack, Stan 83, 101
Harris, Bucky 94
Hartig, Ed 107, 109
Hartnett, Gabby 86–88, 90, 91
"Homer in the Gloamin'" 90
Heindl, Margaret. *See* Popovich, Margaret
Heindl, Violet. *See* Popovich, Violet
Herman, Billy 68, 71, 72, 82, 83, 91, 101
Higgins, Mike "Pinky" 94, 95, 96, 98
Hornsby, Rogers 26, 40, 63–69, 72
Hotel Carlos 28–31, 39, 42, 62, 107–109
name changes 107
Houston Colt .45s (Astros) 98
Hubbell, Carl 84

I

Illinois Masonic Hospital 30, 39, 40
Immenhausen, Herbert G. 35, 41, 43, 49

J

Jensen, Jackie 94, 95
Jurges, Anna (Billy's mother) 24
Jurges, Billy
as coach and scout 92, 93, 99, 100
as minor-league manager 93
Boston Braves 92
Boston Red Sox (manager) 94–98
business career 93
Chicago Cubs (1931 season) 26
Chicago Cubs (1932 season) 23, 26–28, 40, 43, 67, 71, 72, 73, 74, 76, 109
Chicago Cubs (1933 season) 79
Chicago Cubs (1934 season) 79

Chicago Cubs (1935 season) 81–83
Chicago Cubs (1936 season) 83–84
Chicago Cubs (1937 season) 84
Chicago Cubs (1938 season) 85, 87, 91
Chicago Cubs (1946 and 1947 seasons) 92, 93
competitiveness 83, 87, 92, 94, 96, 98, 99, 102
court case 42
death 102
early baseball career 25
love letters 49, 51–52
New York Giants 91, 92
relationship with and shooting by Violet Popovich 23, 30–43, 52, 62, 109
sense of family 79, 92, 98, 100, 102
youth 25

Jurges, Frederick (Billy's father) 24, 28
Jurges, Mary (Billy's first wife) 77, 78, 99, 102
Jurges, Phyllis (Billy's second wife) 102
Jurges, Suzanne (Billy's daughter). *See* Price, Suzanne
Jurges, William Frederick. *See* Jurges, Billy

K

Killebrew, Harmon 99
Kitty Davis Cocktail Lounge 52, 53
Koenig, Mark 71, 72, 77, 78, 109

L

Landis, Kenesaw Mountain 69, 70, 71, 78, 79, 82
Lopez, Al 39, 104

M

Malamud, Bernard 110
Malone, Pat 68, 69
Mathews, Eddie 98–99
McCarthy, Joe 63–66, 74, 90
Moriarty, George 82, 83

N

National League 63, 76, 79, 81, 84, 85, 88, 92, 98, 102
Natural, The 110
New York Giants 83, 84, 87, 91, 92
New York Mets 98
New York Yankees 66, 72–77, 90, 97

O

O'Leary, Charlie 68, 69

P

Philadelphia Athletics 64
Philadelphia Phillies 30, 53, 71, 76, 78, 88, 109
Pister, Jacob 39, 51
Pittsburgh Pirates 43, 67, 68, 71, 81, 83, 88, 90
Popovich, Drogiro (Violet's sister) 55
Popovich, Margaret (Violet's mother) 33, 34, 37, 40, 53, 55, 58, 60, 103, 104, 107
Popovich, Mark (Violet's brother) 55, 58
Popovich, Michael (Violet's father) 34, 55, 56, 57, 60, 107, 109
Popovich, Mike (Violet's brother) 28, 34, 35, 55, 57, 58

Popovich, Milos (Violet's brother) 55, 58
Popovich, Violet
- appearance 23
- burlesque show 45–48
- court case (Billy Jurges) 42
- court case (Lucius Barnett) 51–52
- dance lessons 37, 59
- death 107
- employment 26, 33, 37, 38, 44, 48, 52, 59, 105
- Los Angeles, California 62, 103, 105
- love letters 49, 51–52
- marriages 37, 59
- marriages (Charley Retzlaff) 103
- marriages (Tony Stenella) 33
- relationship with and shooting of Billy Jurges 23, 30–43, 52, 62, 109
- show business career 26, 37, 38, 44, 48, 52, 59, 103, 107
- youth 55–58, 109

Povich, Shirley 72, 74, 87, 95
Prescott, Mark 48, 103–105, 109
Prescott, Michael 105
Price, Bill 100, 102, 103
Price, Suzanne 79, 103

R

Reagan, Ronald 101
Retzlaff, Charley 103, 105
Root, Charlie 73, 74, 76, 82, 88, 89
Ruth, Babe 72, 73, 74, 75, 76, 109

S

Sbarbaro, John A. 35, 36, 40, 42, 45, 49, 52
Seattle Mariners 98
Sopcak, Anna 60
State-Congress Theatre 45–48
Steinhagen, Ruth Ann 109
Stenella, Tony 33
St. Louis Cardinals 81, 83, 85, 88, 92
St. Paul's Evangelical and Reformed Church 39, 51, 57
Subject, Betty 38, 60–62, 109

T

Taft, Charles P. 63
Taft, William Howard 63

U

Uhlich Children's Home 56–58

V

Vanities. See Earl Carroll Vanities
Veeck, William (Bill), Jr. 66
Veeck, William, Sr. 40, 64, 66, 67, 68, 69, 71

W

Waitkus, Eddie 54, 109
Washington Senators 98, 99
Wayne, John 104
Williams, Frederick B. 52
Williams, Ted 94, 95, 96, 97
Wrigley Field 28, 45, 71, 72, 73, 75, 76, 84, 88, 93, 102, 109
Wrigley, Philip K. 70, 71, 86, 91, 93
Wrigley, William, Jr. 63–66, 71

Y

Yawkey, Tom 94, 96, 98

ABOUT THE AUTHOR

University of Mary Washington.

Jack Bales was born in Milwaukee, Wisconsin, and grew up in Aurora, Illinois. His lengthy career in librarianship included more than forty years at the University of Mary Washington in Fredericksburg, Virginia. He has published books as well as numerous articles and essays for books, journals, magazines, literary encyclopedias and newspapers. He is a member of the Society for American Baseball Research, and his initial research on the 1932 shooting of Chicago Cub Billy Jurges appeared in the fall 2016 issue of the *Baseball Research Journal.* "The Show Girl and the Shortstop: The Strange Saga of Violet Popovich and Her Shooting of Cub Billy Jurges" won the McFarland–SABR Baseball Research Award in 2017. His in-depth history of the early Chicago Cubs, titled *Before They Were the Cubs: The Early Years of Chicago's First Professional Baseball Team*, was published in 2019 by McFarland.

Bales retired in 2020 as Reference and Humanities Librarian Emeritus at UMW. He lives in Fredericksburg and is the father of two children, Patrick and Laura. When not researching and writing, he enjoys hiking with them, particularly in the Shenandoah Mountains.